TO

Curran Pool

FROM

EB

DATE

4/17/2022

WHEN JESUS SPEAKS TO A BRAVE BOY

Print ISBN 978-1-63609-064-1

Published by Barbour Publishing, Inc., 1810 Barbour Drive, Uhrichsville, Ohio 44683, www.barbourbooks.com

Our mission is to inspire the world with the life-changing message of the Bible.

Printed in the United States of America.

000973 1021 BP

MATT KOCEICH

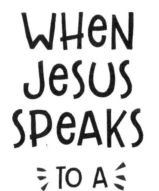

WHEN
JESUS
SPEAKS
TO A
BRAVE
BOY

A DEVOTIONAL

BARBOUR kidz

A Division of Barbour Publishing

Wait for the Lord. Be strong.
Let your heart be strong.
Yes, wait for the Lord.

PSALM 27:14

Listen closely, brave boy. . .
Jesus is speaking to your heart.
Jesus speaks. . .every day
and in every situation!
Listen for His voice as you read
through the devotions in this book.
You'll come away feeling
unconditionally loved and blessed!

Brave Boy,

You mean the world to Me. I want to tell you so many things to remind you how special you are. I am with you every day. You can rely on Me to be there for you in every situation. I am here to bless you with the courage to be brave. I am with you to help you make good choices and treat others like I treat you.

Read your Bible and remember that's how we stay connected. Pray and tell Me what's bothering you. Don't let friends tell you I'm not real. I made you, and I love you. You will always be important to Me. By My power, I will always help you know more of My heart and all the things I feel and think about you.

I have special plans for your life. I know there are days when you don't feel good or you worry about things, but I want you to know that you are loved. I want you to know that more than anything, I died for you so you will have a deep and unique relationship with Me. I want your heart to get to the place where the enemy can never tempt you to forget My promises. All day long, from the time you wake until the hour you close your eyes, I want you to know and love Me even more. Think about all the things you have to tell Me, and let the words of My Book, the Bible, guide your soul. Let them protect your mind from the world's empty promises.

For God so loved the world that He gave His only Son. Whoever puts his trust in God's Son will not be lost but will have life that lasts forever.
JOHN 3:16

DAILY HEART CHECKS

Brave Boy,

I love you more than you will ever know, and I want your eyes to shine as they read My Word. I want you to trust Me and know My promises are true. I want you to get to know Me better every single day. I want you to read and understand My Word so it will guide you in your life and choices. My words can protect and comfort you.

I give you strength to walk away from every wicked thing. I am pure and holy, and I want so much more for you. Don't be drawn to people who don't care about Me or My commands. Do daily heart checks to make sure loving Me is always your top priority. I want you to know more about My holy character. I want you to know more of My heart and all the love I feel for you. My desire is for you to worship

Me with ever-deeper love and praise as your heart opens up to the truths about Me found in My Word.

The enemy wants you to forget that I made you righteous. Brave boy, despite the evil that fills the world, I have planted you by My streams of living water. Stay rooted to Me. I am here to bless you because I love you.

Happy is the man who does not walk in the way sinful men tell him to, or stand in the path of sinners, or sit with those who laugh at the truth.
PSALM 1:1

FOLLOW Me

Brave Boy,

Today, remember that you are My chosen child, dearly loved and forever forgiven. You have been set free! Hear Me say your name, and feel your heart leap for joy at the wonderful gift I have given you. You don't need to try harder or worry about gaining the approval of other people. No! Your inheritance in Me is priceless.

I alone am your strength and courage. By My power you will stand against the enemy's temptations. I am like a rod of the strongest iron that breaks the devil's schemes to pieces, as though they were formed of brittle clay. This is your new reality, brave one. This is the truth. There are so many people who do not believe in Me, but still I reach out to them. Just as I sent the prophets to tell the world that I alone can save people from their sins, today I am sending you to reach the hearts of many who are hurting and weak. Be brave. Tell them that I am the Messiah.

Live each moment of this new day with the generous heart of a servant. I am your example. Follow Me. Share compassion with someone who needs My love. I breathed life into your lungs and opened the eyes of your soul. Let your words and actions join together to celebrate Me!

The next day Jesus wanted to go to the country of Galilee. He found Philip and said to him, "Follow Me."
JOHN 1:43

SAFE BESIDE ME

Brave Boy,

Keep your heart rooted in Me, because I am worthy of every ounce of your life. I want more for you than you could ever dream on your own. I see you. I see when you are having bad days, and I am right by your side. I will not let you face today alone. I go before you, and I stand behind you. I am always here. The problems in your life are temporary, and your problems certainly aren't your purpose. They will pass—and when they do, you will know without a doubt that I was the One who solved them.

I want you to remember this always: *I am here with you and for you.* I know there will be times when you might not feel smart enough or big enough to handle hard things, but those are just lies the enemy whispers in your ear. You are who I say you are. And I made you special! No one else in the world is like you! I want you to be confident, because I am your biggest supporter.

Know that you are safe here beside Me. You can't walk farther than My grace, because My grace has no ending. And you can't outrun My forgiveness, because I said your sin problem is finished! I am a shield around you, and I am always here to lift your head high. Every time you call out to Me, I will answer you.

For by His loving-favor you have been saved from the punishment of sin through faith. It is not by anything you have done. It is a gift of God.
EPHESIANS 2:8

BRAVE AND BOLD

Brave Boy,

I am the One who keeps you going and who gives you rest. I am the One who watches over you while you sleep, and I am the One who wakes you up every morning. Brave one, no matter what the day holds, remember that I hold you. No matter what time it is, I carry you. Let the words of the Bible carry you through every situation. Let My truth help you feel loved and special—just the way I see you. My words will always keep you on the path I've chosen just for you. My plans for you are perfect.

I want you to remember that you never need to be afraid. Even though you can't see Me, I stand guard over your life. I am always surrounding you with mercy, grace, love, forgiveness, hope, and so much more. I constantly shower you with these things so you will always hear My voice and follow it.

As you head out into this new day I am giving you, I want you to be brave and bold. I am here for you. Call out to Me in courageous faith. You are so much stronger than you know. I am with you, and you can rest assured that nothing in the world can separate us. My blessings are forever. I will keep all My promises, because I am your righteous King and I love you.

Who is a God like You, Who forgives sin and the wrong-doing of Your chosen people who are left? He does not stay angry forever because He is happy to show loving-kindness.
MICAH 7:18

SECOND CHANCES

Brave Boy,

I am here. Spend some time today thinking about this blessing. I am good, and there is no trace of bad in Me. I hear every word you speak to Me, so you never need to feel like you are alone. I am so happy to hear your voice. Remember how special you are to Me. When I answer you, it won't always be the way you want Me to answer. But know that I always work to bring about My plans for your life.

Don't let anything pull you away from My loving heart. Keep your attention on Me. Consider My goodness. My glory is wonderful and has the ability to warm your soul. Some days you might wonder if I'm so busy helping other people that I don't know what you're going through. But you can be sure I am with you always, and I love you forever. . .no matter what!

When you spend time thinking about Me and reading My words in the Bible, you will be reminded that I have set you apart. You are My faithful servant, and I am very proud of you. Even when you mess up, remember that I am a God of second chances. You are My chosen child, and I have given you a new heart. You have been made into a new creation and are no longer without hope. You are wonderful because I have made you wonderful!

Who can keep us away from the love of Christ? . . . The world above or the world below cannot! Any other living thing cannot keep us away from the love of God which is ours through Christ Jesus our Lord.
ROMANS 8:35, 39

WHO I REALLY AM

Brave Boy,

Each day I am here to remind you of who I am so that your heart can match Mine. The more you read about Me in your Bible, the happier your heart will be. You will begin to see Me for who I really am. When you lie down at night and when you wake up to a new day, search your heart and make sure My truth is the only thing planted there. Be quiet and listen. Hear My voice guiding you.

Today—and every day—is a new day to worship. With all you do and all you are, point the world back to Me. Let your hands give help to those who need it. Let your feet take you to those longing for My good news. Most of all, trust Me when I say your life matters.

Your heart is always in My hands. I am here to help you when you don't feel well or when you're hurting. I alone am the One who brings real healing. I alone know exactly what you need. I made you to remain in Me and feel the light of My radiant face shine over you. Keep your eyes on Me. Let Me be the One who fills your heart with joy. I am your Peace Giver and the One who enables you to lie down in safety. I know the days can be difficult, but I am the One who cares. Rest in Me, because I love you.

" 'For I know the plans I have for you,' says the Lord, 'plans for well-being and not for trouble, to give you a future and a hope.' "
JEREMIAH 29:11

Brave Boy,

Pray. Talk to Me and tell Me everything. I listen to your words. I understand every sad feeling, and I receive every expression of your worship. Don't let the enemy twist the truth. He wants you to believe that I'm distracted and not paying attention to you. The devil wants you to think I treat each of your prayers differently. He wants you to believe there are easy prayers that I always answer and hard ones that I may not respond to.

Brave boy, please hear Me. I am your King. I don't love just a part of you. I don't care about only some of your dreams. I don't hold half your heart in My hands. When I thought of you and created you, I made you complete and completely for a relationship with Me. *Everything* about you matters to Me. And the same is true about your prayers. Whether you are asking Me for help or lifting up My name in praise, I hear every word.

From the moment you wake up, talk to Me. I have been watching over you as you rested. And just as I wait for you to rise in the morning and pray, I want you to wait on Me to answer you. But don't wait like a person who has no hope. You are My wonderful creation. You are the one I love. You're deeply cared for and chosen by Me. You mean more to Me than you know. I hear your voice. Expect Me to answer all your prayers, because I love *all* of you!

Give all your worries to [God] because He cares for you.
1 PETER 5:7

MINE

Brave Boy,

I want you to learn more about Me every day. I want your thoughts to be always on Me. I look at you, and I see your heart. I am pleased with you. Let your heart beat for Me. Be kind to everyone you meet. Do everything with love in your heart.

The world is full of pride. People want to be first, and they desire to protect themselves from the consequences of their bad choices. That's not who I made you to be, brave boy. Stay humble. I know sometimes it's hard to do the right thing. Run away from bad choices. Don't worry if someone laughs at you or calls you names. Know that I am proud of you. I am always with you and will help you.

Because of My great love, I made a way for you to stay safe in My arms.

Think about Me. Come close, because I made you in My image and that makes you very special. Think about My commands. Let your words bring Me praise, and your actions shine light on My holy name. I have called you "Mine" so that you might spend your days thinking about My wonderful love for you. My words will be the light that guides you through every situation. Show the world how much you care about our relationship by giving Me all of you.

"Do what is right and be kind and show loving-pity to one another."
ZECHARIAH 7:9

NO WORRIES

Brave Boy,

I am here for you. I will lead you through every one of the days I have made for you. I go before you, and I also surround you like a shield on all sides. Use My Word as a map to follow the straight path I have laid out for you. I am so proud of you for trusting Me. You never need to be afraid or worry about things that are out of your control.

My words and My promises are trustworthy. I spread My arms of protection over you so that you are safe and cared for. I know there are days when everything seems to be going wrong and nothing good seems to happen. But don't be discouraged. I am always here to help you. I will always take care of you. When you put your trust in Me, My power lives in you. I live inside your heart, closer than you could ever imagine!

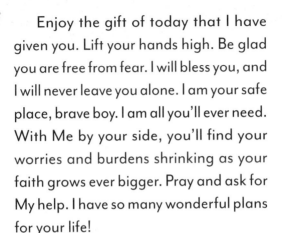

Enjoy the gift of today that I have given you. Lift your hands high. Be glad you are free from fear. I will bless you, and I will never leave you alone. I am your safe place, brave boy. I am all you'll ever need. With Me by your side, you'll find your worries and burdens shrinking as your faith grows ever bigger. Pray and ask for My help. I have so many wonderful plans for your life!

Whom have I in heaven but You?
I want nothing more on earth, but You.
PSALM 73:25

STRONG ENOUGH

Brave Boy,

I love you. My heart is the lens I look through to see you. I want you close, and no bad day can ever pull you away from Me. There will be days when you are hurting or sick. You might feel sad. But trust that My love surrounds you and comforts you even on the very bad days.

I understand how you feel. I know what it's like to be sad. I know what it's like to feel alone because no one seems to understand what you're going through. I know, brave boy, because I died on the cross for the sins of the whole world. I wanted to save *you*, because you are very special to Me. So when your day is long and hard and you call out to Me, know that I hear you and am ready to help!

Don't get discouraged by what your friends might say or do. Run after My love.

Come close to Me. I turn My eyes to you and watch over your young heart. I will help you through the hard times because of My great love for you—and My love for you will never end. My heart is powerful enough to shower you with love even on your darkest days.

The Lord will always lead you. He will meet the needs of your soul in the dry times and give strength to your body. You will be like a garden that has enough water, like a well of water that never dries up.
ISAIAH 58:11

PROMISES

Brave Boy,

I promise to bless you and take care of you every day. I know there are days when you feel worn out. And instead of thinking about Me, you begin to worry about things that are out of your control. But whether you have one problem or a bunch of them, know this, brave boy: *all* of your problems are temporary.

When it seems like you've cried enough tears to make a waterfall, remember that I am here. I will dry your eyes and lift up your head, My beloved child. It's okay to feel sad, but know that I understand. Remember that I care about everything you care about. I am always with you. I always see and hear you. I will always be your strength and protection. I am here to make sure you have everything you need. Let your faith grow strong because of My love.

The hard things you go through in life matter to Me. I am here to help you with your problems. I hear every single one of your prayers! Because of My love for you, this new day will be brighter. Trust Me with today and remember that I will never leave you alone. Your life is precious, and I made you unique. There is only one *you*. Read My words—My promises—in your Bible and be reminded of just how special you are to Me!

And my God will give you everything you need because of His great riches in Christ Jesus.
PHILIPPIANS 4:19

Brave Boy,

Find true rest in Me. I am your Friend, and I care about you. I am here to rescue you. I am here to deliver you from all the problems that are troubling you. Sometimes you may feel swamped by the difficult things in life, but you have nothing to fear. You don't have to worry or be afraid, because I will always save you. So let your heart be filled with hope!

Because I am the Peace Giver and Rest Giver, you can leave every hard thing to Me. Keep your eyes on Me. Let everything you do reflect My holiness. Speak every word with kindness and grace. Let each thought be marked by love. Let your friends see Me in you. You can show them how much I love and care when you don't worry about things.

I offer you My protection. I rise up and

destroy sin. I rise up and keep you safe. Come close to Me. Sing songs to worship Me, brave boy. Put your faith in Me—and turn away from the darkness that the enemy brings into the world. No matter how badly you mess up, I will forgive you! Use the hours of each new day to lift My name high. I am delighted when I see your heart beating for the things that are important to Me.

"Do not be sad for the joy of the Lord is your strength."
NEHEMIAH 8:10

SECURE

Brave Boy,

Your life is secure in Me. I know days will come when I'll need to remind you that I'm not mad at you. . .that I understand your stress and worry. But always remember that I am the shield that protects you. My hands pull you away from harm. I go before you and behind you for your good. I see the minds and hearts of people, so I understand what you think and feel—the good and the bad. I promise I will make every wrong thing right. You can always trust Me.

I am the Warrior who gives you My sword of truth, the Bible. I stand firm against evil. I am always prepared to battle for your heart. As I defend you, I also lead you into pastures of goodness and peace. Brave boy, hope will *always* win. To keep this hope in your heart, read

34

My Word every day. Then you will win against the enemy, who wants to keep you in darkness.

Child, never overlook the importance of having a thankful heart for all the things I've done for you. Show gratitude for the love and hope I have given you. Sing praises for all the blessings I have showered over you. I am faithful, and I always keep My promises. Let your heart overflow with joy. I am your King, the Lord Most High. I am the One who loves you.

Good will come to the [person] who trust in the Lord, and whose hope is in the Lord.
JEREMIAH 17:7

Brave Boy,

Take time this new day to think about My holy name. My name is above all other names. It is grander than anything the enemy tries to sell you. I am here for you. Rest in My arms. I will help you grow into the person I created you to be. I created you in My image, and I want your life to reflect My heart for people—a heart overflowing with love. Hearing My name should bring calm to your soul. . .let it bring you rest.

Look up at the sky. From the rising and setting of the sun to the twinkling of the brilliant stars throughout the night, I Am. Let your voice join the chorus of believers who praise My name.

Brave boy, I also want you to think about the work of My hands. Consider how I have set the sun, moon, and stars in their proper places. In all of My creation, the hearts of My people are what matter most to Me. Caring for you is My priority. I look at you, and I am delighted in you. You are and always will be precious to Me!

"The Lord is my share," says my soul, "so I have hope in Him."
LAMENTATIONS 3:24

Brave Boy,

Every word of thankfulness that springs from your lips is wonderful to Me. I have created you to be a beacon of hope that points the lost and hopeless back to My loving arms. Live today by the beat of your grateful heart. Don't be ashamed to tell the world about Me. The enemy will try to silence you with lies. He wants you to feel depressed. He wants to see you weak and worn out. But the truth is that when you worship Me with every ounce of your soul, the enemy and his defeated armies stumble and slink away.

You are My wonderful child, full of life and hope. Don't let sad times keep you down. Instead, remember that I am always here to lift you up.

I have rescued you for a beautiful purpose. I chose the cross because you mean so much to Me, brave boy. I am your loving Savior, and I rule with truth and goodness. I am a safe place for anyone who is discouraged or brokenhearted. When your mind is swirling with worried thoughts, I am here to be your strength. You can trust Me. I have given you My word: I will never walk away from you. Follow Me, because I will always be true to you.

The Lord your God is with you, a Powerful One Who wins the battle. He will have much joy over you. With His love He will give you new life. He will have joy over you with loud singing.
ZEPHANIAH 3:17

Be BOLD

Brave Boy,

For every dream you hold close to your heart, I am worth even more. For every hurt you may experience, My love makes a way for you to go on. Let your life be a song of praise for all that I am. Be bold and tell the world about all the blessings I've given you. Remember, the enemy wants you to keep it all to yourself. He doesn't want you sharing the Gospel. The enemy wants you to stay quiet and run after everything the world says will make you happy.

If you're waiting on an answer to prayer, it doesn't mean I haven't heard you or that I'm far away, focused on something or someone else. The enemy would love for you to believe that I am too big and you are too small, so there can be no way for us to connect. But that just isn't true. Brave boy, find your worth in Me, and don't listen to the devil's lies. You can hear Me speak with your heart. You can feel My love and grace when the impossible happens. I am here right now to hold you and hear you and bless you.

Spend time singing praises to Me. Let your heart rejoice! I will *never* forget about you or ignore your needs. When hope seems lost, remember that I am here to rescue you. I am the One who keeps you safe and renews your hope, because I love you.

Hope never makes us ashamed because the love of God has come into our hearts through the Holy Spirit Who was given to us.
ROMANS 5:5

Seek Me

Brave Boy,

I am right here by your side. I am never far away. When the enemy whispers that I am walking away from you, don't listen. He will try to convince you that you're all alone every time trouble comes your way. The devil will try to keep you distracted from Me—and focused on mistakes and bad choices. The enemy wants to discourage you and steal your joy.

I want the opposite for you, brave boy! When trouble arrives, I will stand between you and the problem so you can see only My love and goodness. You are forgiven. Talk to Me today. . .right now! Don't let pride get in the way of all the blessings I have for you. There are so many gifts I want to give you, but first you have to make room for Me in your heart and in your thoughts. Keep My

42

commands close to your heart and obey them. Find Me in the little things. Find Me in your daily routine. You can see Me in every single aspect of your day, because I never leave you.

Don't worry about the things you don't have right now. Don't worry about things you think you should have. I care about you, and I will provide everything you need. My love for you is the best gift of all. With My love surrounding you, you can focus on all the good things in life. You can give Me all your worries. Brave one, let Me carry you. Let Me shelter you from every storm.

"No eye has ever seen or no ear has ever heard or no mind has ever thought of the wonderful things God has made ready for those who love Him."

I CORINTHIANS 2:9

PRAY!

Brave Boy,

I want you to talk to Me as your very best Friend who loves you deeply. Pray to Me with all your heart. Call out to Me. I am ready to hear everything you have to say—good and bad. Go ahead. . .I'm listening! Lay all your worries and troubles at My feet. Then get ready to be amazed by the way I will answer your prayers.

I am here to take care of you in times of joy and times of sorrow. I am your King who sees and knows everything. I feel your sadness, brave boy. When you are upset, I want you to know that I can—*and will*—comfort you. Continue to give your life to Me. Because of My love for you, your life will shine like the sun. Nothing can take you away from Me.

I am the King, Lord of heaven and earth. In Me there is no darkness or spot of sin. In Me there is no shame. I hear your prayer. I know what you want and need most. Be encouraged. For today, tomorrow, and forever, I am your holy Lord. I am your eternal Defender, spreading My arms of protection over you. I love you, and you are Mine.

"I am all you need. I give you My loving-favor. My power works best in weak people." I am happy to be weak and have troubles so I can have Christ's power in me.
2 Corinthians 12:9

YOUR Refuge

Brave Boy,

Run into My arms. Take shelter. Let Me
fight all your battles for you. Don't be
lured into looking for comfort in worldly
things. The enemy wants you to run after
man-made solutions to conflict—but that
never works! Brave one, hear My voice:
I have already conquered your sins! You
are debt-free—I have paid it *all* for you.

The enemy watches Me as I stand
guard over you. He wants to trick you into
believing his lies. He quietly whispers that
you aren't really saved. . .that I don't really
love you. He suggests that you are not
really Mine because you make mistakes.
But you are Mine because I said so! You
are saved because I took all your sins to
the grave! The enemy sees Me blocking
his evil lies. He will *never* take your soul
out of My hands! Continue to resist the

enemy's lies with My help.

I am on My throne, and My passion is for everything right and good. Use this new day to be brave for Me. I love justice, and I love you. Stand tall and remember that one day soon you will see My face! Until that wonderful day, let your light shine.

We have this light from God in our human bodies. This shows that the power is from God. It is not from ourselves.
2 CORINTHIANS 4:7

MY AMBASSADOR

Brave Boy,

Many people you meet don't have faith in Me. But don't worry. Remember, courageous one, that your worth is not in their words but in Me alone. Be an example. Let your friends know that I am the only Answer and My love is all they will ever need. Be the one who cares for people who are angry and hopeless. Show them My love and light.

When you see people who need Me, brave boy, I will silence the voices that tell you you're too young to make a difference. Today is for *you* to share Me and My love. I am calling you to be My bold ambassador and to speak My truth to those who need to hear it. I am your Savior who will defend the hearts of others too. I am Lord over all the earth. I am the Lord who hears. I alone provide victory over sin and evil.

My words and the commands I give you are perfect. I made you, and I know your needs. The instructions for your life that you find in the Bible are for your good. I speak to you through the scriptures. When you stop and listen, your life is changed for the better—every single time. Though the enemy will try to lead you away from Me, I will always keep you safe by My side.

The Lord is my strength and song. He is the One Who saves me. He is my God and I will praise Him. He is my father's God and I will honor Him.
Exodus 15:2

THE ANSWER

Brave Boy,

I know you have many questions. I know life feels overwhelming sometimes, and you wonder if I might have forgotten you. But My love overcomes every bad thing. When the enemy lies and tries to convince you that I won't answer your prayers, say, "Jesus is my Answer. He is all I need!" When the devil distracts you with sad or scary things, say, "Today I choose to focus on Jesus!" When it seems like the evil one is winning, say, "My God already won the battle for my heart!"

Trust Me to give you the best answer to each one of your prayers. I keep My eyes on you. I'm looking ahead, to places you can't see, to make sure you will be out of harm's way. I will always protect you from the enemy's tricks and traps. He will never win, because I am the One who paid the ultimate price for your heart.

Through every situation you face, trust in Me and My unfailing love. In good times and in hard times, let your heart rejoice. Praise Me for who I am. Let your heart beat for the things My heart beats for. Know that I am holding you through every smile and every tear. Even when the hurt seems too big, I am holding you and will never let go. Brave boy, your heart is safe with Me.

"Have I not told you? Be strong and have strength of heart! Do not be afraid or lose faith. For the Lord your God is with you anywhere you go."
JOSHUA 1:9

WORLD-CHANGER

Brave Boy,

The world doesn't have the right answers. So often, instead of running to Me and taking shelter in My love, people live in fear. Then the enemy makes their fear even bigger with his lies. He makes people think that sinful anger and hate are acceptable. But you know better, don't you? I am calling you to be a difference-maker. Brave boy, be the one who stands up for Me.

It doesn't matter how young you are. You can change the world! I made you and gifted you to do amazing things. Let today be the day you let your faith in Me rise. Let your love for Me inspire you to do something big. When you begin doing big things, be on the lookout, because the enemy will try to discourage you. But I am telling you the truth: I will give you the strength and courage to be a world-changer!

Go into the world and tell your friends, family, and neighbors about Me. Tell them about the name of Jesus. Tell them I am here—right now! Tell them I will keep them safe. Tell them I am here to comfort and heal. Don't be afraid to show the world how I've made a difference in your life, brave one. I am so proud of you for not being ashamed of Me!

The Lord is faithful. He will give you strength and keep you safe from the devil.
2 THESSALONIANS 3:3

Brave Boy,

I made you to go wherever I go. The enemy wants you to feel like I'm far away in heaven and you're alone here on earth. But you need to know that My presence is with you *always*. Wherever you go, I am there. Think about this truth today, and let it fill your heart with hope. Walk with Me and depend on My strength to live a good, wonderful life. Give to others from My overflowing love for you. Let others see Me through your kind and caring ways.

Think about other people first. Treat them with respect. Serve them with a generous heart, and love them like I love you. Use your words to lift people up. Don't put up walls to keep people out. Speak kindness and get rid of anger. Keep your promises. Respect My mighty

54

name. Let people see Me in everything you say and do.

No matter what the world says, *nothing* can destroy My love for you. I will never let the enemy shake your faith in Me. Give your time, talent, and treasures to help others without expecting anything in return. The evil one will try to convince you that you should only help others if you get something from it. This idea couldn't be further from the truth. Go out into the world today and share My loving-kindness!

The Lord God is my strength. He has made my feet like the feet of a deer, and He makes me walk on high places.
HABAKKUK 3:19

ALL YOU NEED

Brave Boy,

I love you. I am your King, and I will keep you safe in My mighty hands. When the enemy sneaks around, trying to plant lies in your heart, I will put a stop to his evil plans. I am always here to protect you. Trust Me today for *everything*. I am all you will ever need. I shed My blood for you, brave boy, so rejoice in My holy name!

Take some time today to think about all the things I've done for you. Treat others so well that they want to get to know Me too. Show them that a relationship with Me is better than anything else in the world. Satan wants people to believe they can be happy without Jesus. . .that the world is enough. The way you live your life can show others that true joy comes only by walking with Jesus.

The world is watching you. They are watching how you treat your friends and family. They are watching to see how you act when life is hard. They are watching to see if you behave the same way during the week that you do at church. And with My power working through you, they will see Me, your Provider. I am enough. Through Me, your salvation is secure. You are My child, and I love you!

The Lord is my light and the One Who saves me. Whom should I fear? The Lord is the strength of my life. Of whom should I be afraid?
PSALM 27:1

Brave Boy,

Your life is secure with Me. I have planned many wonderful things for you. Follow Me to beautiful green pastures and rejoice because I have given you a delightful inheritance. I have set boundaries in place to keep you safe and on the right path. Even though you may not want to follow My rules sometimes, they are for your very best. Don't get so distracted with chasing your dreams that you forget to listen to My instructions.

Keep your eyes on Me. I love you and provide for you. I am always by your side. Because of My love, your heart can be happy. Rejoice and celebrate because of all the blessings I have given you. Rest in Me, knowing My hands hold you close. Remember that My power fills you with the strength to do the right thing and make good choices.

Most of all, brave one, I want you to know that I will never abandon you. I have already given you the gift of eternal, forever life. I will fill your heart with My presence. Because I have saved you, you now walk on the path of life and your heart beats with My joy. I can't wait to show you My plans for your life! I love you!

I have placed the Lord always in front of me. Because He is at my right hand, I will not be moved.
PSALM 16:8

HONESTY

Brave Boy,

I hear your prayers. I hear your praises and your pleas. I hear every word. I am your best Friend, and I care about you. Look inside your heart. Are you hiding anything from Me? I want you to give everything to Me. Part of My character is honesty—truthfulness. When I say something, it is 100 percent true. And I want the same from you, brave one. I made you to have a relationship with Me. And that means sharing whatever you think, feel, want, and need.

Listen to My voice. Read your Bible and hear Me speak directly to your heart. My Spirit will guide you and teach you all the lessons I have for you. Give Me all of you, so I can give you more of Me. I have plans for all your days. I designed you to become the person I created you to be—not what the world says you should be. The enemy wants you to be okay with the ways of the world. He wants you to ignore Me.

Throughout each day, make time for Me. Ask Me about My plans for you. Walk the paths I want you to walk, and I will not let your feet stumble. I'm not asking you to do these things on your own. Brave one, I made you, so please let Me be your everything. Let My great love for you be your daily treasure.

"You will know the truth and the truth will make you free."
JOHN 8:32

LOVED BY ME

Brave Boy,

Don't look to the world for answers. Don't listen to the enemy's lies. From the very first moments in the Garden of Eden until right now, the devil has been lying to human beings. And he is skilled at convincing humans that lies are the truth. He will tell you to do whatever you want, but the truth is this: I am everything you need. The devil will tell you to take care of everything all by yourself, but the truth is this: I made you to be loved and cared for by Me.

Be the courageous one who stands up against Satan's lies. Show the world what My name really means by the way you show them more of Me. Hold My name high above the lies so others can see what real hope looks like. Let your life show the world what it means to be fully loved by Me. Speak truth and let your praises to Me be the key that opens hearts to My love.

I look forward to the day when you will see Me face-to-face. Trust the promises I make to you. While you're waiting for Me to return, living your life for My purposes, I will protect you. When you feel overwhelmed by sadness, I will rise up and bring you joy. When you feel worn out or afraid, I will be right there with outstretched hands, waiting to save you from life's storms. When you are tired and feel powerless to take another step, I will be there to carry you. Let My love be your hope!

We have come to know and believe the love God has for us. God is love. If you live in love, you live by the help of God and God lives in you.
I John 4:16

YOUR ROCK

Brave Boy,

I know you love Me. And I love you. No matter what! But the enemy wants you to feel like you have to perform, or pretend, to earn My love. That's not living My way! The gift of life I've given you is just that: a gift. You can't earn your salvation by acting like you have it all together. No. You just need to rely 100 percent on Me. I am your *everything*. I am your strength, so you don't have to try to be strong all on your own. I am your rock, so you don't have to pretend like you're not afraid of anything. When hard times come, remember that your life is anchored to Me. Nothing will take you away from Me. You don't have to act like things are fine when they're really not. I am the One who can save you from every stressful situation. Just ask Me for help!

The enemy wants you to feel like you will never be good enough for My love. He hopes you will always feel "less than." Most of all, the enemy wants you to completely forget about Me. But together, we can put a stop to his lies.

Today, tomorrow, and forever, I know exactly what you need. I'm not far away from you, occupied with other things. I am with you. All day, in every moment, I am with you. I am your rock. When heavy thoughts make you feel alone and scared, I am there to remind you just how much you matter to Me.

**Jesus Christ is the same yesterday
and today and forever.**
HEBREWS 13:8

GRACE SETS YOU FREE

Brave Boy,

Today I want you to spend time thinking about My never-ending love for you and what I did to save you so that you can spend forever in heaven with Me. When hard times come, remember My promises to you. When you make a mistake, remember that I will erase it forever, if you just ask Me to! When you feel like you're just an ordinary kid, remember that I made you—and when I did, I made you special! Because of My love, you have been set free. You delight My heart, brave one!

I'm never mad at you—even on your most terrible day. . .even when you make a super-bad decision or big mistake. I give you My love every single day, and I have made My home in your heart. I know you will never be perfect, but that won't undo My love for you. There's nothing you can do to make Me love you more, and there's nothing you can do to make Me love you less. Your doubt will never be able to diminish the storehouses of mercy I have to give you.

I will always protect you from the enemy's lies. He doesn't want you to know how much you mean to Me. He doesn't want you to know you are forgiven. The enemy wants you to see Me as a mean judge, not your loving Savior. Don't believe his lies. Instead, rejoice in the truth that I chose to rescue you! Worship Me with a thankful heart today. I love you!

From Him Who has so much we have all received loving-favor, one loving-favor after another.
JOHN 1:16

BIGGER THAN ANYTHING

Brave Boy,

If you're having a hard day, look for something good. Today is an opportunity for you to do wonderful things, and I am your biggest supporter. I have already won the battle for you. I have overcome all your trials and all your problems. So instead of focusing on the bad stuff, see today as an opportunity to move closer to Me. Open your Bible and learn more about Me and who I am. I know focusing on only good stuff can be hard. I know you'll have days that seem to be filled with one problem after another. But trust Me, brave one. Know that I am here, helping you get through it all one minute at a time.

I made you to feel joy. I don't want to see you overwhelmed by sadness. I delight in you, and I want to watch you enjoy the day I've given you. When you asked Me into your heart, you were saved at that very moment, and I made you free. Free to have joy in your heart no matter what happens each day. When the enemy tries to convince you that nothing I say is true, tell him to stop! Say a prayer quickly, and I will comfort you and remind you of My promises.

Rest in My peace. Live free. Ignore the enemy's lies. Follow Me. I won't turn away from you, brave boy, so remain by My side. Nothing in the world can change who I am, so don't waste one second believing that you are anything less than who I say you are. You are My child. You have been forgiven, and I love you.

Jesus said, "Let the little children come to Me. Do not stop them. The holy nation of heaven is made up of ones like these."
MATTHEW 19:14

Brave Boy,

I am faithful. I will never let you down. Just in case you've forgotten. . .I am the One who listens to your prayers. I am your shield and support. I never go back on My word. I keep every single promise I make. And today is an opportunity for you to become more like Me as you grow in your faith. So spend some time with Me. Read My words in the Bible. Listen to Me even more today than you did yesterday.

What you read about Me in the Bible is true all the time. I am the same—I never change. I will always be the One to encourage you. I will always be the One who cares about everything you're going through. I am with you always.

My Name is holy. I am pure and perfect. And I have made a way to save you. If you haven't already, just ask Me into your heart. I will turn all your darkness into light. I will protect your heart from the enemy's tricks. Let My love make you courageous and strong. With Me by your side, you will do all the amazing things I have planned for you to do!

If we tell Him our sins, He is faithful and we can depend on Him to forgive us of our sins. He will make our lives clean from all sin.
1 John 1:9

Brave Boy,

My plans for you are perfect—and that's a promise from Me to you! I'm not just saying this to make you feel better; I'm telling you this so you are full of hope for your future! With Me, you are safe. With Me, you are strong. With Me, you are wise. With Me, all your tomorrows are full of opportunity and adventure!

When it seems like nothing is happening, listen for My voice. Listen to Me and learn from My words. I will lead you in the way you should go. Your Bible is truth, and it will show you how to live and love others well. I use My Word to strengthen you. My Word will always guide you in the right direction.

My love for you will never go away. I won't bless you today and then take away My blessing tomorrow. The enemy will tell

72

you that time spent with Me is nothing but rules to follow. I offer you so much more, brave boy. Follow Me to understand who I am and who you are in Me. Read My words and let them sink deep into your heart. Let My truth grow inside you and help you realize how much I love you.

But You, O Lord, are a covering around me, my shining-greatness, and the One Who lifts my head.
PSALM 3:3

I AM LISTENING

Brave Boy,

I hear every word you speak, and I take each one seriously. I am always listening. When you feel sad, My strength will lift your spirit and bring you joy. My love for you takes your requests and turns them into answered prayers. I keep every promise to you, because you are precious to Me.

Today is a gift. It is a blessing for you to receive and appreciate. When you live each day with a grateful heart, your friends will notice and begin to wonder about Me. They will want to know about the powerful love that rescued you from sin. Some will even give their lives to Me because of your example. Brave one, you have My kingdom-bringing power. Your life matters.

Let your life show the world that I am God. Let your actions remind the world that I am your rock. Let your friends, family, and neighbors hear you praise Me. They will know that I am your Protector. They will see how I guard your heart. They will see how I save you from days filled with sadness. They will see that you are My child. Let My never-ending love fill your heart today. I will give you the courage you need to shine like the brightest star on a dark night.

Jesus spoke to all the people, saying, "I am the Light of the world. Anyone who follows Me will not walk in darkness. He will have the Light of Life."
JOHN 8:12

THE RIGHT WORDS

Brave Boy,

Don't be discouraged. Look up, and you will see that I am here for you and will never leave you. Everything I made for you to enjoy bears the mark of My love. Every star. Every sunset. Every ocean. Every mountain. I love creating beautiful things. And you, brave one, are worth more to Me than all of them combined. With your life, tell the world about My love. Fill your days and nights with praise for all I have done. Worship Me and keep your heart focused on My goodness and grace.

I am your guardian. I fight for you. I am the keeper of your soul. Just as the mountains, which have no voice, speak of My glory, so does your life. Don't worry about finding the right words to speak about Me. I will give you the right words.

My love for you is active. It seeks you

out and finds you, no matter where you are or what situation you're in. Because of My love, everything will be okay. If you're angry or mad, happy or sad, I am with you. Like the sun, My love for you rises in the morning and shines on you all day long. No part of today (or any of your tomorrows) will be outside of My love for you.

Those who belong to Christ will not suffer the punishment of sin.
ROMANS 8:1

YOURS!

Brave Boy,

My words are true. My directions are right and good. Following My instructions in the Bible will bring joy to your heart. I will help you to see people as I see them—through a heart overflowing with love. I have good plans for all your days, brave boy. Spend some time today reading My Word. Open your Bible and let the scriptures speak to your heart.

I want you to treasure My words. They are worth more than gold because they will last forever. My words will open your mind and heart. My words will help you to discover great blessing and hope. My words will help you stand strong against evil. My truth is what leads you away from darkness and into light.

Keep your eyes on Me today, brave boy. I am the One who made you blameless—

I am your Savior who has removed the stain of sin from your life. I have washed your heart and made it new. I am your safe place. Your Redeemer. Your salvation. Your hope.

I will say to the Lord, "You are my safe and strong place, my God, in Whom I trust."
PSALM 91:2

Brave Boy,

I will answer you when you pray to Me. I will do even more than you ask because I love you so very much. My name is powerful enough to protect you. I don't want you to be lonely or to go through hard days on your own. Being with you through each of life's storms is one of the ways I show My love. Keeping My strong hands under you to support you is another. I am the keeper of all your days. You will be with Me forever, brave one!

When you make giving a priority, you make more room in your heart for Me. When you let go of the world's treasure, I will fill your empty hands with blessing upon blessing. You can trust that I am the One who is worthy of all your praise. I alone will give you all the hope you need. With Me, you are free to let go of selfishness and pride.

Today, give Me all your plans. Trust Me with all your wishes. Live each of your days with a joyful heart. Let your words and actions show the world that I am your King. I am listening to everything you are asking Me to do. Trust Me. I love you and will do only what's best for you.

Every word of God has been proven true. He is a safe-covering to those who trust in Him.
PROVERBS 30:5

TRUST

Brave Boy,

Hear My heart beat for you. Listen to My voice speak over you. Pay attention to My words and think about them today. Remember you are My child. I have chosen you. I have called you My own. You have been redeemed. Your sins have been forgiven, and your future is secure. Don't worry about anything, because I will be with you for all your days. My plans for you are perfect. I am going before you to make your path straight. No matter what you feel, you will be victorious when you do the work I am calling you to do.

I have answers to all your questions. I will help you understand what you mean to Me. Remember, I am always with you. There isn't even a minute when I leave you alone. I am giving you the strength to take your eyes off the world and put them on

Me. Stop trying to make things go the way you think they should, and instead let Me take control of every part of your life. Rise above life's cares and concerns and stand firm on My promises.

Trust Me. Trust in My holy name. I love you, brave boy!

You will keep the man in perfect peace whose mind is kept on You, because he trusts in You.
ISAIAH 26:3

A MIGHTY SAINT

Brave Boy,

Spend time today thinking about how My strength helps you. Let My power bring you joy! My strength carries you, not only when you're weak, but even on your brightest, strongest days. My strength enables you to stand up for what's right and share My truth with others. Don't listen to the enemy when he tells you that you're too young to make a difference. You are a mighty saint, and you are very important to My kingdom.

First thing every morning, brave one, talk to Me! I will help you discover new truths as you read your Bible. You will find more of who I am in its pages too! I am here for you. I listen to you. I answer your prayers. It's you and Me, together for all eternity. I am filling your heart with My love so you can face this new day with

84

confidence. You are right where I want you to be.

Rest in Me. Take comfort in My presence. I love you. Let this truth bring you never-ending joy as you live out your day. Keep your trust in Me and not in the ways of this world. My love for you never fails, and it will always keep you strong.

"We have the Lord our God with us, to help us and to fight our battles."
2 CHRONICLES 32:8

Brave Boy,

My desire for you is that you would know more of Me. I want you to feel My special love—a love that helps you understand how important you are and how much you mean to Me and others. Today I want to remind you of My power and protection. I know how easy it is for you to get tired. Even when your days are packed with activities and tasks that drain you of energy, I walk by your side to help you. I plant joy and strength in your heart.

Every word in the Bible was breathed into existence by Me. I made sure My words were recorded in the Bible so you could feel My presence. I did it so, no matter where you are, you can not only read the scriptures but *feel* My promises. I take the responsibility of keeping you safe very seriously. When the enemy comes near, I prepare for battle. I will protect you, and together we will win!

Take this new day and use it for praise. Let your words and actions overflow with worship. I want you to practice doing for others what I am doing for you. You are more than capable because you have My power to serve others and to do so much more. I am holding you in My arms and never letting go!

For the Lord will be your trust. He will keep your foot from being caught.
PROVERBS 3:26

New Life

Brave Boy,

Please trust all My promises. I am with you always. I will never leave you all alone to defend yourself. From the moment you invited Me into your heart, you were completely saved! And My promises to you never change. But the enemy will whisper that I have gone away and left you to save yourself. He wants you to feel scared and worried, but I will rescue you from the things that bring you down.

Brave one, you are completely My child. All of you belongs to Me. No part of you belongs to the world. Even your mistakes will not take you away from Me. You are wholly loved and wholly wonderful, even when you struggle to believe it. But trust Me always.

You have been made brand new. When the enemy tries to distract you from

Me with the things of the world, pray for strength to resist his temptations. I am so proud of you. I know the days can be hard, but keep your trust in Me. I am your Deliverer, and every part of you—inside and out—matters to Me!

For if a man belongs to Christ, he is a new person. The old life is gone. New life has begun.
2 CORINTHIANS 5:17

Brave Boy,

Remember that your worth is in Me. You are not who other people say you are. You are not who the enemy says you are. You are more than a good person who tries hard. You are not weak. You are not a disappointment to Me. You are not hopeless. You are not ignored. You are not forgotten. You are not a failure or a waste. You are not insignificant or help-less. And you certainly are not a mistake.

   Who you really are is found in My heart—it's how I see you. Your worth is found in the truth, and the truth is this: you are wonderful! You are loved and completely forgiven. You are free. You are powerful. You are hopeful. You don't have to earn My favor, because you are Mine and I love you. You are fully known and adored. You are a success. You are important to Me. You are special. You are significant and helpful. Just as you delight in Me, I delight in you. I've had amazing plans for you since I first thought of you and created you in your mother's womb.

The truth is, I love the person you are. So today, let's celebrate. I've made worship to replace fear, so lift up your hands and praise Me, for I am worthy.

"Do not be afraid, just believe."
MARK 5:36

Brave Boy,

Sometimes, as soon as you feel connected to Me and My promises, the enemy will lash out. He hears you thank Me for a blessing and immediately jumps into your thoughts to create a distraction. Just as soon as you feel My love fill your heart, the devil is there to try to steal your joy. His lies are strong, but don't be afraid, because I Am. I am bigger. I am stronger. I am wiser. I am in control. And I am. . .love.

There will be times when we'll share a powerful moment and then the enemy will seem to drain you of all hope. Just when you use My strength to move a mountain, the enemy causes another one to come crashing down around you. Just when you feel My arms surround you, the devil threatens to take My comfort away.

The enemy will use a lot of tricks to

confuse you, but the simple truth is that I am Love and I understand what you're going through. I will always show you what's right. Keep reading your Bible. Follow My commands. Let My words of truth make you stronger. Believe Me when I say the devil is powerless to take you away from Me. Little one, call out to Me, because I am listening.

God. . .will give you strength. He is the God of all loving-favor and has called you through Christ Jesus to share His shining-greatness forever.
I PETER 5:10

YOUR BIGGEST SUPPORTER

Brave Boy,

I am here for you all day, every day. In fact, I was with you even before you were born. As you grow, I will ask you to do many things for Me. And I will always give you the strength you need to do them. Whenever you need My help, I will be quick to respond. I want you to always have hope in your heart because of My love for you.

I am your biggest supporter. I celebrate your life because you are Mine. Don't be bothered by things that are out of your control. Let Me continue to teach you how amazing you are and how important you are to Me. And remember that I am never far away from you. When I say that I am your strength, I mean that you are capable of mighty things because of Me. You can rely on Me all the time.

Don't be frustrated. Don't let the

enemy take over your thoughts by telling you I am never going to answer your prayers. I've told you before, and I will remind you over and over again, that *all of you* matters to Me. I do not hide from you when you pray. No! I shower you with grace and carry you through every moment of every day. I will answer every prayer, so don't fear. While you wait, let your heart be filled with more of My love.

My body and my heart may grow weak, but God is the strength of my heart and all I need forever.
Psalm 73:26

IMAGINE

Brave Boy,

I am the reason you can stay hopeful in the middle of hard things. Continue to trust that I will keep My promises, even in the middle of your darkest days. I am the One who satisfies your desires. I alone give you what you need. Read My words in your Bible and listen to My voice guide you through every minute of today. Keep Me as the focus of your praise. Worship Me through your words and actions. Let your friends, family, and neighbors see a difference in your life so their eyes may be turned to Me.

No matter what the enemy says, I love you, brave one. No matter what lies he tells, I am proud of you. I have set you free! Imagine all the wonderful things I can do through you if you just believe!

Put forth your best effort today.

Remember Me and the love I give you day by day, moment by moment. I am your King. Take the truth of My Word to the world. Ask Me to show you the neighbors or friends who don't yet know Me. Help them see My grace. Invite them to join you in worship. Show them that My heart is worth more than all of earth's treasures combined. Help them see that I alone will bless them. Don't be afraid to proclaim My Name to the world. I am with you, and you are Mine!

God is able to do much more than we ask or think through His power working in us.
EPHESIANS 3:20

THE JOURNEY

Brave Boy,

I am your Shepherd. I will lead you to lush green pastures so you have everything you need. Trust Me. Follow Me. I am taking you on a journey that I planned just for you. Along the way, I will look out for you. I will stand watch over you. I will provide time for you to rest. I know there are days when you feel so very tired, but I am here to renew your strength. I will con- tinue to guide you beside quiet streams of water. My love for you is constant and unending.

I have rescued you from darkness. Now that you are set free, follow Me as I guide you along paths of righteousness for the sake of My holy name. As you follow Me through each new day, I will show you more and more of who I am. Even though some days will be filled with struggles, I will always make a way for you to know and feel My love.

I care about you so much that even during hard times, you will have peace. Just lean on Me. I provide for your every need. I shower you with blessings. Stay here with Me, brave one. Here with Me you are surrounded by goodness. Rejoice, because you are My child today and forever. I love you.

The Lord is my Shepherd.
I will have everything I need.
PSALM 23:1

SAFE AND FOREVER LOVED

Brave Boy,

Everything in the earth is Mine—I created all of it. I made the oceans and mountains, the land and skies. My power that created these things also breathed life into your lungs and opened your eyes and made your heart to beat. You are very important to Me. You are My wonderful child. I created you special. Nothing—no matter how big it is—can overshadow My love for you. Be joyful because you are chosen. You live under the shadow of My wings. You are safe and forever loved.

The enemy wants to get in the way of you and Me and My promises—and he is very good at waiting. He waits for you to get tired and worn out. I will help you resist him. Call My name. I will strengthen you and bless you, child.

Spend this new day with Me. Read My

words. Let each one of them sink deep into your heart. My power will give you courage and peace. Whether you're at home or out in the world, look up. You'll see My love. I am the Almighty One. I am your King, and I love you.

"O Lord, you are great and we fear You. You keep Your agreement and show loving-kindness to those who love You and keep Your Laws."
DANIEL 9:4

Brave Boy,

There is only one Me. My name is "Wonderful." I am the only One who is Peace. Trust Me. I keep your heart safe. I will not let you down. I have made you to win in life!

Follow Me and I will show you the plans I have for you. Follow Me and listen to My voice. Stay in My Word. Let My commands be your guide through today and all your tomorrows. You can always count on My truth. Keep hoping in Me all day long. As we walk together today, I want you to know that I fill up your heart with peace and love. I forgive you for all your sins. Just talk to Me. I'm waiting to hear your voice, brave one.

Remember that I am righteous. I am full of grace. I am with you *forever*. Listen to Me, and I will teach you even more about My amazing plans for your life. Don't let hard times come between you and Me. It is in the hard times that I am closest to you. I am loving and kind and faithful to forgive. When you ask, I'll wash your sins away. Today shine for Me. Today do great things for My sake. Today know without a doubt that I love the brave boy I made you to be!

Give all your cares to the Lord and He will give you strength. He will never let those who are right with Him be shaken.
PSALM 55:22

THE ONE WHO GUARDS YOUR HEART

Brave Boy,

I am your Teacher. I guide you in every area of your life. I will show you the right paths to take. Doing life all by yourself is hard. Doing life with Me by your side is so much better! Read My Word—in it I share My promises with you. I keep every one of them. Rely on Me and not the world. The world will disappoint you and let you down.

When you keep your eyes on Me, I give you freedom. As you plant My words in your heart, your feet remain on My right paths. I offer a never-ending supply of grace. I'm reminding you of these truths, brave one, because I know the devil's tricks. He tries to convince you that you are all alone. He whispers in your ear that sadness and hard times are what I want for your life. The truth is that loneliness and sadness come from living in a broken world. But there's good news! I take your beautiful heart and remove all the loneliness and sadness it holds. . . and replace those things with My joy!

I watch over you. And when I look at you, I see My chosen child and not a sinner. When you asked Me into your heart, I rescued you and made you into a brand-new person. I am the One who guards your heart. You are worthy of My love. Never forget that! You are Mine.

"See, I am with you. I will care for you everywhere you go. And I will bring you again to this land. For I will not leave you until I have done all the things I promised you."
GENESIS 28:15

NO FEAR OF FALLING

Brave Boy,

Did you know that you never again have to worry about falling or failing? And it's all because of My never-ending love. Rely on My faithfulness in all things. My mercies are new every single morning. I have good plans for you because you are precious to Me. I never grow tired of reminding you of My love because I *never* grow tired of you. I will never walk away from you. I will walk beside you all the days of your life.

Stay near Me and let My promises comfort and encourage you. Make choices that are in line with My Word. Don't get wrapped up in the ways of the world, brave one. I want your choices, words, and actions to praise Me. In this way, you are sharing Me with the world. Even though you are young, I have called you to be a leader. I have called you into a close relationship with Me and not the world.

Ask Me what My will is for your life. And love everything that brings Me glory. The enemy will be persistent and keep trying to pull you away from My grace. But you are My child. You have been saved and set free. I love you, and My hands will hold you forever!

Men become right with God by putting their trust in Jesus Christ. God will accept men if they come this way. All men are the same to God.

ROMANS 3:22

THE POWER OF MY LOVE

Brave Boy,

Think about My love for you. I have strengthened you with My mighty power, so you never need to be afraid—of anything! I am protecting you every minute of every day. When your day seems hard, remember My promise, and don't let your heart be burdened. I am with you. I will make you brave.

Use My strength to pray when you feel weak or unsure. Ask Me to come close to you and make you feel safe. Use My words to fill your heart with truth. When your heart is focused on Me, you will find the courage you need. Read your Bible and memorize verses that make you feel brave. My Word is the key to discovering the treasure of My love and care for you. My words will guide you into a deeper relationship with Me.

Even with Me close, you will make mistakes from time to time, but don't let your weaknesses keep you from trusting in My power to forgive. I hold you in My arms, and My grace for you abounds. I will always forgive you, brave boy. I love you today, tomorrow, and all your days to come.

But whoever obeys His Word has the love of God made perfect in him. This is the way to know if you belong to Christ.
1 John 2:5

NEVER LETTING GO

Brave Boy,

Tell Me everything. Give every thought and dream to Me. I hear you, and I will answer you. Always look to Me and not the world for answers. I created your heart to beat for Me. When you need Me, just look up. I am here to fill your heart. My love will never fail. When the world lets you down, you will hear My gentle voice tell you that you're loved. When the enemy tries to attack your faith, you will hear Me whisper, "You're Mine. I'm never letting you go."

I will never hide from you or ignore you, brave one. I'm so very proud of you. I made you in My image, and I never make mistakes. In life you will have disappointment from time to time, but remember that *you* are *not* a disappointment to Me—not ever! I know there will be days when you question My plan for you, but remember and trust that I know your heart even better than you do. No matter what, I will always do what's best for you.

Listen to Me. I will teach you how to stay on the straight path. Remember not to run ahead of Me—just walk beside Me. If you ever do get ahead, wait on Me. Look and you'll find My goodness, even on the hardest days. No matter what you feel, I make you strong. You are My dearly loved child.

God is faithful.
I Corinthians 10:13

JOY!

Brave Boy,

Keep your heart always wanting more of Me. Remember that I am your rock. My comfort and protection are for you. I know you sometimes worry that I won't answer your prayers. I know you get frustrated when you think I'm being silent. But trust that I will answer every single request in My own timing—and My timing is always perfect. When you're in doubt, read My Word for reminders of My love for you. I will fill your heart with pure joy.

I will help you accomplish all the plans I have for your life. I am in control of all things. And I am Judge over all things. You can trust Me to fulfill every promise I have made to you. I am righteous, and I am the source of all your happiness.

I am your everlasting strength. No matter how weak or helpless you may feel, I am always holding you up. I will keep your feet from stumbling. I will protect you from the attacks of the enemy. And I will never stop helping you. I will never stop loving you. Keep trusting in Me, because I am worthy. I am not just Mercy and Peace. I am not just Grace and Forgiveness. I am also your Fortress of Salvation. I have saved you, and today I am blessing you. And My blessings will bring you joy that lasts forever!

You will show me the way of life. Being with You is to be full of joy. In Your right hand there is happiness forever.

PSALM 16:11

Small Steps

Brave Boy,

Your life brings Me glory. Watching over you brings Me delight. The enemy would love for you to take your eyes off Me and instead focus on your problems. But tell the enemy, "No!" Then turn to Me. Each small step you take toward Me is important. Keep your eyes on Me, and you will see My strength. You will see how I hold your life safely in My hands. The truth is that I am in control of every single thing—including you, brave one. And I have an amazing future all planned out for you. You can look forward to wonderful days ahead!

Each day I will remind you of My goodness. Just watch the sun rise in the morning and set each night. Feel the cool wind on your face. Listen to the crickets chirping their songs. I created the beauty of this earth just for you. Every blessing is yours to enjoy, so don't hesitate to say My name in praise and thanksgiving. I am your King, and you belong to Me. You are Mine forever.

If you listen in the quiet, you will hear My voice. It will bring comfort to your soul. My voice will light your path and show you the right way to go. As you go about your busy day, make time for a quiet conversation with Me, brave one. Even on the loudest days when it's hard to hear, My voice will break through the noise. Be still, and you'll hear just how much I love you.

O Lord, I know that a man's way is not known by himself. It is not in man to lead his own steps.
JEREMIAH 10:23

Brave Boy,

Today is about your journey with Me. I love you and want your love for Me to grow ever deeper. Your life is worthy because I created you and you are special! You can be sure My words are true, because I am the Promise Keeper. When you asked Me into your heart, I saved you. Every time you call out to Me, I bless you with good things. You are so important to Me. Keep living your life with love. You can do this by having a servant heart.

When you feel weak and tired, rest in Me. Remember that I will handle all your worries and cares so you don't have to. Don't get distracted by looking ahead and trying to control your future. Don't waste today by worrying about tomorrow. Slow down. Walk with Me. Talk with Me. I know, brave one, that many things in this world can distract you from Me. But don't let those things take away your hope. In Me you have peace and security. With Me by your side, you are unshakable.

Consider everything I have done for you. I hear all your prayers. I never stop helping you. I turn your sorrows into joys. I forgive all your sins and clothe you with righteousness. You are free. So today, let your heart sing. Don't keep Me all to yourself! Give others the gift of truth—the gift of getting to know Me too.

If anyone wants to keep his own life safe, he will lose it. If anyone gives up his life because of Me and because of the Good News, he will save it.
MARK 8:35

STRONG FORTRESS

Brave Boy,

You're always safe with Me. Today grow closer to My heart while you share My love with the world. I will lead you to those who need to know Me. Don't be embarrassed or ashamed. I am your strong fortress, so be bold. Do the work I am calling you to, and blessings will follow.

Everything you do, do it for Me. Follow Me and you'll experience more blessings than you could ever wish or hope for. Let Me be the One who saves you from hard things. I will be there through every up and every down. You can count on Me. Don't put your hope in earthly things. Don't rely on other people. Trust in Me. Hold tight to Me. With Me, you'll be satisfied and loved every day of your life. When no one else understands you, I do.

Find your worth and purpose in Me.

Hide yourself in Me. I will give you rest when life is stressful. I will set you free. I don't want you to worry about anything or to fear anything. I am in control. When you feel tired and weak, I give you energy. I will always give you what you need to get through your days. Even when grief comes and you feel lonely or sad, I will comfort you. Don't settle for anything less than My unfailing love. It fills your heart and reminds you how special you are to Me.

The name of the Lord is a strong tower. The man who does what is right runs into it and is safe.
PROVERBS 18:10

I HEAR YOU

Brave Boy,

I am in control every hour, every minute, every second of every day. Trust Me when I say you have nothing to fear. I keep watch over you. I will save you with My unfailing love. I know you have prayed prayers that seem to have gone unanswered by Me. I know you still have dreams that haven't come true. I love you, brave one, and I promise that you *will* hear from Me. I haven't forgotten you. Today—and every day—I hear you. I care about you. Be patient while you're waiting to hear from Me.

I have an abundance of blessings for you, so don't let others and the world bring you down. Just ask Me, and I will free you from the distractions of the world—from all the things that try to keep you from Me. Ignore the hurtful words of others. Those words have no meaning when they don't tell of your worth in Me. I am always here to build you up and speak words of blessing over you. My love and compassion for you are never-ending.

I have wonderful things planned for your life. Remember, you are not a mistake. Keep your hope in Me, and don't let the enemy's lies work their way into your thoughts. I am never far away. I am right here with you—always. And when I am with you, I am making you strong. Continue to be faithful to Me, and feel My power fill your heart. Be strong because that's what I created you to be!

We are sure that if we ask anything that He wants us to have, He will hear us.
1 JOHN 5:14

Brave Boy,

You are blessed because you are forgiven. You are blessed because I love you. Your mistakes won't keep us apart from each other. Day by day, you are becoming the brave young man I made you to be. Today—and every day—continue to live in My presence.

The enemy wants you to spend your time on things that don't matter. He wants you to think you need to handle everything all on your own. He wants to break your trust in Me. Don't fall for his tricks. Instead, put your trust in Me. I will carry your burdens and give you My strength. Be honest with Me and let Me know what you're thinking. Share your feelings with Me. I made you to rely completely on Me for help.

You are never alone in dealing with

life's problems. Brave one, the truth is that I have made you to praise Me. I have made you to be not only My hands and feet but also My voice to the world. Reach out to your family, friends, and neighbors. Who needs to hear about Me? Remain faithful to My will for your life, and know that I am your safe place. I surround you with My love and protect you. Follow the guidelines in My Word, the Bible, all your days. Be glad because you are Mine. I love you!

"Before they call, I will answer. While they are still speaking, I will hear."
ISAIAH 65:24

Brave Boy,

Be joyful. Worship Me today. Worship isn't just for church on Sunday mornings. You can praise Me all week long! When you sing praise songs and listen to My words, you will feel My presence and your heart will fill with My love. After all, I created you to praise Me. I made your hands to be raised high in worship. Have a grateful heart for all the blessings I give you. Let go of your burdens—give them all to Me.

Did you know that I created you to be a leader? I made you to stand up for what is right and good. Share My truth and lead your friends, family, and neighbors to Me. I will be faithful to help you do what I'm asking you to do. When you're tired, I will give you rest. When you feel sad or worried, I will remind you of My unfailing love. Look around you and you will see

My fingerprints on everything.

I spoke and the heavens were created. I breathed the stars into existence. And I have given you life. My love surrounds you. At My command your life is protected and your path secure. The dreams I have in My heart for you will never be shaken.

Our hope comes from God. May He fill you with joy and peace because of your trust in Him. May your hope grow stronger by the power of the Holy Spirit.
ROMANS 15:13

CHOSEN

Brave Boy,

I am with you every minute of every day. I care about each one of your needs—big and small. I want you to connect with Me. I want to be your best friend. You are My child. Morning and night, I watch over you and keep you safe. You are blessed, and I have chosen you. I promise that I will always love and take care of you.

I am the One who saves you and gives you strength. I am more powerful than you can even imagine, and I never take My eyes off you. So, brave one, keep hoping in Me and My love. I care for you today, and I will care for you forever. I will meet all your needs.

Because you are Mine, I will protect you. I will help you succeed. No matter how strong you are, you still need Me. You might have days when nothing seems to be going right. On days like this, I will give you hope and joy. Trust Me to keep My promises. Continue to chase after Me. Find Me in every hour of the day. Trust that I care. Believe that I love you—*always*.

Jesus said. . . , "You must love the Lord your God with all your heart and with all your soul and with all your mind."
MATTHEW 22:37

SUN AND STORM

Brave Boy,

I am the best promise keeper there is. Do you know why? It's because I love you so much. You are My priority. When I give you big blessings, you can bless others too. When you give to others, you are giving to Me at the same time. Cherish every minute of your day as a gift. Each new day is My gift to you, brave one. Each day is a new chance to grow even more into the amazing young man I created you to be.

It doesn't matter whether the sun shines or lightning strikes. No matter what happens today, I am with you. . .I will answer your prayers. I made you to spend time with Me, both now and forever. You shine bright in this dark world when you keep your focus on Me. Whenever you need Me, night or day, I am there for you. There is no trouble I can't save you from, so follow Me today with fresh faith in My promises.

Look for Me in everything you do. Find all the comfort and rest you need in Me. I am a good Father, and I am here for you. Don't forget that whether you're happy or hurting, I am with you. Seek Me and gain strength from My presence. Come to Me and remain in My love. Remember that even on dreary days, the sun is still shining in your heart.

"This cannot be done by men but God can do anything."
MARK 10:27

DREAMS

Brave Boy,

You are safe in Me. I made you to live a life that brings Me glory and gives you peace. I created you to love life, not just get through each day. I want you to follow your dreams—and I will be with you every step of the way! The enemy wants you to believe you're hopeless and that your dreams will never come true because I'm not big enough to make them happen. Brave one, each day that I give you comes from My good heart. And each day is a blessing and gift that allows you to be with Me and learn more about the loving God I am. Always chase after My goodness. You'll never regret it.

Don't forget that I am always watching over you. I am always looking ahead and behind, making sure your walk with Me is protected. I listen to you. I hear everything you say, and every word matters. The light of My Word is always there to guide your steps. I am never against you. I won't ignore you or walk away from you. I will never leave you to face your battles on your own. I am right here with you, and I will deliver you from every one of your troubles.

When you're feeling sad, don't forget that I am right here to restore your joy. I lift you up and hold you close. Even though you will have hard days sometimes, I am with you and will deliver you from all of them. I will be your rescuer.

**Trust your work to the Lord,
and your plans will work out well.**
PROVERBS 16:3

WAIT ON ME

Brave Boy,

I am the mighty Warrior who protects you. The reason I can tell you not to worry or fear is that I am right here with you. No matter what trouble comes your way, I stand ready to defend your heart. I stand between you and the enemy so he will fail every time he tries to distract you from Me. Take this new gift of today and rejoice in Me. Celebrate how much I love you.

There is no one like Me. Nothing in this world can satisfy you like I can, because I created you. I am the One who rescues you when life feels too hard. I am the One who defends you when the enemy tries to steal your hope. I will not leave you alone to be sad. No. I will lift you up and give you what you need. I am good—I saved you so you can have a forever home in heaven with Me.

You can be sure your prayers to Me never go unanswered. Listen and you will hear Me direct your steps. When you stumble, I will catch you before you fall. I am so pleased with you, brave one. Don't be afraid even when you feel as if the whole world is against you. There is never a time when you are not protected by My love. Wait on Me and I will show you the great plans I have for your life.

Let them call out for joy and be glad, who want to see the right thing done for me. Let them always say, "May the Lord be honored. He is pleased when all is going well for His servant."
Psalm 35:27

DEEPLY LOVED

Brave Boy,

Please don't worry what other people think. Don't let their opinions change the way you see Me. Listen to what I say about your worth. No matter what kind of day you have—good or bad—spend every minute rejoicing and giving Me thanks. I have called you My dear child, but you are also My friend. You are loved and filled with My peace and truth. And that is all that truly matters. Remember, I am the only One who gave up My life for you.

I know what you're going through. I know exactly what you're thinking and feeling. I have told you before, and I will remind you over and over again, that I will never leave you alone. I will never walk away from you. I will never leave you wondering where I am. I am your Defender. I hold your heart in My hands.

I will show you that your life matters.

I care about you. You are very valuable to Me. I am asking you to live a life that shows others My love. There are people who don't know Me like you do. Be bold and tell them about Me. Love people the same way I love them. Speak kind words to those who are hurting. When you do, you will show them how much they mean to Me.

**You are of great worth in My eyes.
You are honored and I love you.**
Isaiah 43:4

Brave Boy,

Don't worry what other people think of you. Don't let their words define you, because I define you! Don't forget that when your day gets stressful, I keep loving you. I will help calm your heart. You matter to Me, and I have a good plan for your life! The world will hear you praise Me and share My words of truth. They will see you do good things from your brave heart. They will watch as you serve and love others the way I do. They will learn from your wonderful example!

My love and faithfulness touch every part of your life. I give you confidence to stand up for Me in this fallen world. My goodness and mercy are deeper than the deepest oceans. No matter where you go, I am there. I give you hope and hold you close to My heart. I give you meaning and purpose. I guard your heart and soul with

My love that *never* fails.

My blessings for you go on forever. I never look at you and hold back blessings because of your mistakes. Instead, I look at you and am pleased with the wonderful creation I made you to be. Through Me, you will discover the plans I have for you. My love for you will never end. It continues to fill your heart and give you hope and joy. My presence keeps you strong and safe. Follow Me today. Hear My voice say you are important and dearly loved!

"This city will make My name known. It will be to Me joy, praise and shining-greatness before all the nations of the earth that hear of all the good that I do for them. And they will fear and shake because of all the good and all the peace that I give it."
JEREMIAH 33:9

LIGHT COMES FROM ABOVE

Brave Boy,

When life seems dark, look up. That is where you will see My light. I was with you yesterday. I am with you today. And I will be with you tomorrow. Nothing can stand between us. You are safe with Me by your side. Take time today to be still before Me. Know that I am alive and working to fulfill the plans I have for you. Be patient while I show you the best way to live your life. Get rid of the darkness with the light that comes only from Me.

Trust Me, child. I always know what's best for you. It's good for you to spend time doing kind things for others. Whether you listen to someone who needs to talk or give your free time to help a person solve a problem, do it all for My glory. I love you because I *am* Love. Let Me fill your heart until it overflows with love and contentment. Listen to Me and follow My best plans for you. My Word is truth. And My truth will bring light and joy to your life.

Keep hoping in Me. Keep talking to Me. Obey My Word and I will give you peace. Know that I am never far away. If you run after Me, I will bless you, brave one.

"See! I see heaven open and the Son of Man standing at the right side of God!"
ACTS 7:56

Brave Boy,

I don't want today to be a burden. I want it to be an opportunity for you to grow ever closer to Me. Know that whatever the days brings, I alone am your help—I have the solutions to all your problems. Stand firm on the rock of My Word, the Bible. Good days and bad days. . .I am with you through every one!

Read My words. Think about My truth. Follow My commands. I made you to do great things for My glory. I am your Shepherd, and I guard your life so you never have to worry. My words are powerful weapons against difficult things. Reading your Bible will give you the ability to fight and win! As you read, memorize verses. When you hide My Word in your heart, your entire being will be filled with My comfort, hope, and joy.

Brave one, I am always here for you. When you have Me and My Word, you have all you'll ever need. Happiness doesn't come from big, expensive things. Things won't last, but My love will never end. I am worth more than all the world's treasures combined. I have made you new, and I love you, brave one!

Not only that, we give thanks to God through our Lord Jesus Christ. Through Him we have been brought back to God.
Romans 5:11

DOING GOOD

Brave Boy,

Your worth is in Me and Me alone. You can be confident that I am with you every step of the way. My strong hands are holding you and guiding you all day long. There is never a time when I let go and leave you to find your own way. So rejoice! My grace has rescued you from darkness. When you're tempted to look in other places for safety and hope, remember that I am your strong tower.

Spend today doing good for others. This is My plan for you. I am the Way, and I am leading you on the path of justice. Follow Me and be blessed. Keep My commands in your heart. Let them direct your thoughts. Speak truth and know I am protecting you every hour of the day. I will always guide you in the right direction so you can continue doing the work I've called you to do.

No matter what, find your hope in Me. Stay on the paths I have laid out for you. Tell the truth. Always do the right thing so others can see a difference when they look at you. Be peaceful. Tell your friends, family, and neighbors about Me. Tell them, brave one, that I love them and came to rescue them too.

He brought me up out of the hole of danger, out of the mud and clay. He set my feet on a rock, making my feet sure.
PSALM 40:2

DON'T WORRY

Brave Boy,

My love for you is huge! It's so big that nothing can take you away from Me. When I look at you, I see a new creation, perfectly formed by My love. When I think about you, I don't shake My head in disappointment. No. Instead, I see your beautiful heart filled with My mercy and grace. When you live your life close to Me, I make you strong. With Me in your heart, your soul shines light into the world.

Don't get stuck feeling bad because you make mistakes. Instead, talk to Me. Just ask, and I will forgive you. I will give you freedom and hope for all your tomorrows. I will take all your burdens away. With Me you never have to do life alone. On the day you believed in My holy, mighty, and perfect name you were forever set free from the weight of sin.

Because of My salvation, you can experience joy and light every day of your life. Be grateful for My blessings. Sing praises to Me with all your heart.

I am so proud of the young man you are becoming. Never let anyone tell you that you don't matter, because you *always* matter to Me. I love you!

"Which of you can make yourself a little taller by worrying?"
LUKE 12:25

RUN AFTER ME

Brave Boy,

Satan will try to trick you into believing that I never speak to you. . .that My voice is too quiet to be heard. But he speaks nothing but lies. He would like for you never to talk to Me. When your day gets difficult and you begin to feel alone, call out to Me. Just say My name and wait for Me to answer you. I care about you—each and every part! While you're waiting for Me to answer, read My Word. Memorize Bible verses. Remember all the ways I've blessed you. I promise an answer is coming. And I promise that when I answer, you *will* hear My voice.

Every day I celebrate you. Every day I want you to be near My heart. Every day I want to keep you safe. And every day I want you to feel joy. Open your heart and let Me carry your burdens. I remind you of these things so you will continue to run after Me.

Keep walking down the path I've created just for you. I will fill your heart with love and light. Don't be disappointed or sad, thinking that I don't care or that I'm too far away to help you. I promise that I will always be right here with you. I am holding you through every minute of every day. I love you.

So give yourselves to God. Stand against the devil and he will run away from you.
JAMES 4:7

MY TREASURE

Brave Boy,

You are My treasure. I want you to know how special you are. I created you to do amazing things for Me and My kingdom. In the times when I'm calling you to lead, I will give you power and direction. In the times when I'm calling you to love, I will give you courage. I will make you generous and kind. I am the source of everything you will ever need. When you're unsure, I will give you the right words and make a clear path.

Each day I give you is a gift wrapped with My love and grace. Keep your hope in Me, and remember that I will never leave you alone. The people of this world rush around trying to find the next thing to fill their hearts. Brave one, don't get caught up in this game. Instead, rush after Me! Get caught up in *My* plans for your life.

I have carefully designed all your days, and I have blessed each one. I am here to show you the way so you never have to wonder if you're on the right path.

Take each step with Me by your side. Remember My truths in the pages of your Bible. Obey My words. And never forget that I hear and care about every single one of your prayers. Never stop praying. On days when your spirit is full, I give you the strength to lift your hands in praise. And when your spirit feels empty and you think you have nothing left to give, I pour more love into your heart. You are priceless to Me!

And now, Lord, what do I wait for?
My hope is in You.
PSALM 39:7

PERFECT TIMING

Brave Boy,

Wait for Me. Don't let hard things distract you from My loving-kindness. Pay extra attention to My words in your Bible. Don't forget that I saved you. Whatever happens today, you can trust Me and know I am here for you. Brave one, I have planned so many good things for you. Don't be discouraged. I am strong enough to carry you and all your burdens.

Know that you have My full attention. You don't need to do anything special to get My eyes on you. My love and care for you will never stop. Remember that I am the One who opened your heart to salvation. I am the One who made a way for you to have a forever life in heaven. Everything I do and all My promises are because I love you. Trust that My timing is perfect. I hear all your prayers, and I will answer them.

Keep My words hidden like a treasure in your heart. Let My words give you the courage to share My love with the world. Remind the people around you to follow Me. Tell them that My love is great. I think of you all the time, and I keep your heart full of My love and joy. Whatever you need, just ask Me, and I will provide it. Never forget how important you are to Me!

But God showed His love to us. While we were still sinners, Christ died for us.
ROMANS 5:8

Brave Boy,

Look out for friends, family members, and neighbors who are weak. Give them your time. Give them your attention. I will be with you along the way and help you through each difficulty. I will protect you and give you strength and courage as you serve others. When you help the hurting, I am always there to bless you. Reach out to people who are lonely and sad and share My love with them. Make sure they know how much I love and care about them. You are close to My heart, brave one. Don't ever doubt My promises.

Sometimes you will make mistakes. Don't worry—I will erase them. All you need to do is ask Me and I'll forgive you. When you stumble and fall, I will help you stand up. I'll heal your pain. I will make your heart rejoice. Instead of

152

seeing each day as a tough challenge, look at it as a chance to receive more of My love. You are never alone in your struggles. Don't spend a minute worrying when you can give everything to Me and know I'll handle it.

When you fully trust Me, you can turn your focus to serving others. You, brave boy, are My hands and feet to this broken world. I will give you all the strength and courage you'll need. Every morning new mercies from Me fill your heart and keep you from doubting My presence. I am with you forever!

"Give, and it will be given to you. You will have more than enough. It can be pushed down and shaken together and it will still run over as it is given to you. The way you give to others is the way you will receive in return."

LUKE 6:38

★ 153

Brave Boy,

Leave all your worries and cares in My hands. Let everything go, and I will comfort you. I am always with you. Make today's goal to learn more about Me and get to know Me better. I am your King, and I love you more than you could ever imagine. I alone give you hopes and dreams, brave one. I have placed each one in your heart. And if you let Me, I'll show you how to accomplish them too. Anywhere you go today, I am here for you.

Did you know there's nothing you could possibly do to make Me run away from you? Use the light I have placed in your heart to shine and share My message of hope with the world. Live in such a way that others see Me when they look at you. Whenever you feel unsure, look to Me.

Keep hoping in Me, brave one. I have

all the answers you need. I have all the love you need. I did not create you to worry or fear. I made you to shine like a star. I made you to follow Me and praise Me with all your heart. Expect Me to show up in your life today. Expect Me to bless you and show you just how important you are to Me. Hear My voice say that you are wonderful and worthy. You are Mine!

"One of your men makes a thousand run away. For the Lord your God is the One Who fights for you, just as He promised you."
JOSHUA 23:10

I AM STRONGER

Brave Boy,

I am the One who cares for you when times are tough. Some days will overwhelm you. When the noise of the world is too loud and gets in the way of your quiet time with Me, know that I still hear you. Every day keep looking to Me. Know that My love for you is unending. In the dark and in the light, I hear your voice call out to Me. Let Me show you today how much you mean to Me. Hear My voice call you Mine. Even when the world seems to be crashing over you like mighty ocean waves, I am stronger and I will save you. I will protect you in every storm.

I made this new day for you, brave one. I am leading you. I am here beside you. I direct each one of your steps with My never-ending love. Even in the night,

My love and hope are with you. I will bless you, child.

I will never forget you. How could I? You are Mine. I have good plans for your life, and I will be by your side to guide you and give you all the strength and courage you need. I will always make sure to remind you that your worth is in Me.

Live with love as Christ loved you. He gave Himself for us, a gift on the altar to God which was as a sweet smell to God.
EPHESIANS 5:2

TELL THE WORLD

Brave Boy,

I am your biggest supporter. I will always defend you. You are loved and known. You are never alone. Remind yourself of these truths by keeping My words planted deep in your heart. Let Me teach you something new today. Let Me show you how you can be a leader and share My love and truth with others. Did you know that the more you give to others, the more blessings you will receive? It's true!

I am your strength. On those days when you feel weak, I will lift you up. I love you so much, brave one. I created you to be My light-bearer. And I made you to receive My faithful care. The light I've placed inside you and the care I send your way will always give you strength to get through each day. My strength is what makes you brave.

I am with you always. Because I make My home in your heart, you never go anywhere without Me. I am with you when you wake up. I am with you at school. I am with you at sports or music practice. I am with you when you get ready for bed. I am even with you when you sleep! Keep your hope in Me. I cheer you on and celebrate you. I can't tell you enough how much you matter to Me.

"I tell you, everyone who makes Me known to men, the Son of Man will make him known to the angels of God."
Luke 12:8

ALWAYS GOOD

Brave Boy,

Listen to Me. In My Word, I have given you commands and promises. You are My creation, and we share a special relationship. I used My hands to form you and give you life. I care about you so much that I will stay close by your side in good times and in bad. When the things of this world try to distract you from Me, I will never stop working to recapture your focus. Turn your face to Me. Trust that I am always good and want nothing but the very best for you.

I am your King and your Shepherd. I have rescued you from sin and darkness. I have set you free so you can praise Me every hour of every day. I guide the direction of your steps. I light the way for you. I help you to live up to the potential I have placed within you. Don't put your trust in things. Things will always fail you. Instead, keep your trust in Me.

The enemy will still try to make you believe I have turned My back on you. He will try to make you feel powerless and alone. He will try to make you think I have abandoned you and you have no hope. Reject these lies. Hold on to My promises. Remember that I chose you. You have been set aside to shine. Take My hand and follow Me. I love you, brave one.

We are citizens of heaven. Christ, the One Who saves from the punishment of sin, will be coming down from heaven again. We are waiting for Him to return.
PHILIPPIANS 3:20

MAKE A DIFFERENCE

Brave Boy,

Your life matters to Me. I sacrificed My life so yours could be saved. I shed My blood so every one of your sins would be forgiven. Let this truth soak in, because when you fully believe it, nothing can make you feel "less than," unloved, or unwanted. The truth is, brave one, I do not make mistakes. And what I see when I look at you is wonderful. . .priceless. In you, I see a vibrant spirit with so much to give. In you, I see a strong heart that beats for truth and grace.

Today, I challenge you to use the love and strength I have given you to make a difference in someone's life. A caring act can be enough to remind a person of My presence in their life. As you serve others, keep your heart turned toward Me, and never forget how much I love you. This is the path I am calling you to walk down today. No matter what distractions the enemy puts in your way, stay brave. Keep your eyes on Me.

I am your loving heavenly Father, and I hold you in My hands. You live in the middle of My grace and forgiveness. I know your heart, and I am pleased with you. Continue to live for Me all your days. I am with you always. My love for you never fails!

For You are good and ready to forgive, O Lord. You are rich in loving-kindness to all who call to You.
PSALM 86:5

Brave Boy,

Be still today. Let My words sink into your heart. Let My commands make you bold and brave. Share My love and truth with your friends, family, and neighbors. Sing of My faithfulness. Share My goodness with those who need to know Me and experience My love. I have filled your heart with grace and righteousness. I will give you courage to stand up for My name when others around you do not. Use your hands and feet for My glory, brave one. When you pray, pray for the needs of others. Guide them to Me. My saving grace will redeem their souls.

I have blessed you. I will continue to bless you forever. Focus on important character traits like honesty, humility, and justness. Keep your heart rooted in My words so that My truth will shape your life. Keep reading your Bible so My commands will continue to lift you up and protect you from the world's temptations. When you make My words a priority, you will remain humble. You will make a difference in the world.

Be brave. Obey My commands. Never stop seeking Me in prayer. You might not always get what you pray for, but I am always in control. I love you, child. I'm proud of you. I delight in watching you grow into the brave young man I made you to be!

"The Lord gave and the Lord has taken away. Praise the name of the Lord."
JOB 1:21

Brave Boy,

When I look at you, I see a wonderful person. You bring Me delight! Be the person I created you to be. You have been made into a new creation, and I make My home in your heart. Listen to Me. I will always tell you what's right. I will never lead you down the wrong path. Your worth and identity are found only in Me. Honor Me with right living. Honor Me with your words. Honor Me with your love and kindness. My gentle voice will remind you that you are precious to Me. When you feel sad, please know that I will bring you joy again.

I am your King. My love will enable you to reach out and change the world for My glory. Honor Me with your love for others—even the ones who seem to be against you. Realize that others look to you for guidance

166

because they know your help comes from Me. As you bring glory to My name, I will give you overflowing blessings.

Starting in your own neighborhood, begin today to make My name known across the world. My plans are for you to be brave and bold as you tell others about Me. If you're feeling nervous about sharing Me with your friends, family, and neighbors, talk to Me. I will help you. Lean on Me when you feel weak—that's what real bravery is all about!

But there will be no more heavy hearts for those who were suffering.
ISAIAH 9:1

LET ME TAKE CARE OF YOU

Brave Boy,

I am the One who loves you most. I am your safe place, your strong fortress. Come to Me in both good times and bad. I am always with you. With Me in your life, you never have to worry about solving problems on your own. You and I, we're a team! I go before you to make your path straight. Yes, you'll encounter problems from time to time, but I will be with you to help you get through them.

All the strength and power you'll ever need come from Me. Even on those days when everything seems to be falling apart and you're not sure what to do, I am here to protect you. Bad days don't happen because I've walked away from you. No! Bad days happen because the world is broken, child. Remain in Me. Let Me take care of you.

Give all your struggles to Me and then forget them! Hard times are temporary—here today and gone tomorrow. And I am more powerful than all your struggles combined. Even in times when your faith in Me feels shaky, don't despair. Know that I love you. Even in times when your hope seems to be slipping away, don't give up. Everything will be okay, because I never stop keeping My promises to you!

Honor and thanks be to God! He has not turned away from my prayer or held His loving-kindness from me.
PSALM 66:20

Brave Boy,

Don't ever doubt My love for you. I will love you forever. Remember that I am the Almighty One. I am strong enough to handle any problem you'll ever face. I am your Protector. In Me, you are safe. I guard you against hopelessness and fear. Read My Word. Discover all the times I have given My children strength to overcome hard things. Stand tall today on My promises and know that I am holding you safely in My hands.

My plans for your life are better than anything you could ever hope or dream. Trust Me. Spend your day sharing all the ways I have blessed you. Be bold. Tell others how I have been faithful in keeping My promises. As you obey My Word, be encouraged, knowing that I am your Defender. I will never send you out into the world alone. Listen to My voice. I will always remind you that you are strong enough because of Me.

Be still. Quiet your heart. Study your Bible and learn more about who I am. Know that I am the One who cares about you more than anyone else does. I will answer your prayers. See that I have kept every single one of My promises to you. Understand that I am powerful enough to stop your heart from doubting. You are strong in Me, child. I love you!

But the Lord favors those who fear Him and those who wait for His loving-kindness.
PSALM 147:11

PROMISE KEEPER

Brave Boy,

I am the Promise Keeper. Your prayers will never go unanswered, because I love you, child. Look at the pages of Scripture and you'll see how deep My love really is. I am preparing an eternal heavenly home for you. As I bless you today, call out to Me with praise because I am your King. I delight in hearing your joyful song.

Let everything you do today bring Me glory. From this moment until night-time, focus on worshipping Me. As you worship throughout the day, people will take notice. They will hear your words and see your hands reaching out to help the needy. Others will begin to wonder about Me, and you can tell them all about who I am. Go out into the world and be a blessing to others who are looking for truth. Tell them that I am here. . .that I love them and am ready to save them too!

Don't be afraid of anything. My love keeps you brave and secure. Let My Word guide each choice you make. I have chosen you to do great things for Me and My kingdom. You are very important, and you are dearly loved.

Our Lord Jesus Christ and God our Father loves us. Through His loving-favor He gives us comfort and hope that lasts forever. May He give your hearts comfort and strength to say and do every good thing.
2 THESSALONIANS 2:16-17

CONTENTMENT

Brave Boy,

No matter what things you already have, you'll always want more. It's human nature. But things will never make you feel happy or complete—at least not for long. The truth is you'll never be content without Me in your life. I am the One who provides everything you'll ever need. I am worthy of your heart, child. I paid the price so your sins could be washed away. I made a way for you to be brave and stand up for My name.

Look around at My beautiful creation. See the colors of the sunrise and feel the heat of the sun. Look at the mountains and how they rise to touch the sky. Feel the cool breeze against your cheek. My power can be seen everywhere, brave one. Spread the joy you get from My creation throughout your whole day.

When you're having a bad day, think about everything I made for your enjoyment. Which part of My creation do you like best? I offer you peace and contentment, hope and joy. Let this truth guide and comfort you today. Share it with others. I will take your life to amazing places when you seek Me with your whole heart. Rely on Me forever.

"If My people who are called by My name put away their pride and pray, and look for My face, and turn from their sinful ways, then I will hear from heaven. I will forgive their sin, and will heal their land."
2 CHRONICLES 7:14

FAR BEYOND

Brave Boy,

Have you ever been sick and just wanted to feel better? Have you ever been sick and prayed for Me to heal you? Child, know that My love and care for you go far beyond anything you can understand. I am with you when you're healthy, and I am with you when you're sick. Trust that no matter what, everything is going to be okay. Your life is safely in My hands, and nothing will ever take you away from Me.

You'll have days when you wonder where I am—especially if you're not feeling well and want to feel better right away. But know that I hear your prayers. I see you, and I understand how you feel. I am here to bless you, to protect you, and to encourage you.

Trust Me. Trust that I am in control. Trust that I can help and comfort and heal. My love for you is forever, so praise Me with a grateful heart. Let your praise for Me be heard to the ends of the earth. No matter where you are or who is nearby, praise Me. The world is watching, so let all of your life show them My love.

A man came to Jesus with a bad skin disease. This man got down on his knees and begged Jesus, saying, "If You want to, You can heal me."
MARK 1:40

KNOW MY HEART

Brave Boy,

Continue to be humble and serve others, regardless of who they are or where they come from. Continue to be a light for Me. Share Me and My love with everyone. See others the way I see them. Appreciate the differences in all human beings. Every single person has value. Let your heart be filled with My truth. This way, everyone will know you are Mine.

Listen to My words. I will instruct you in the ways you should go. You will never regret following My plan for your life. Read your Bible every day to continually deepen your understanding of My goodness and My heart for all people. Let your hands carry My love to a hurting world. And let your feet move others toward the cross.

Take time today to be still and hear

My voice. Pay attention as I teach you more about the plans I have for you. Listen closely as I tell you more about My limitless mercy and grace. The more you know about My character, the less you will worry about things you can't control. As you continue to read your Bible and learn about My great love for you, find strength in every one of My promises. Understand that trusting Me is what reminds your heart that I am your ultimate treasure.

But as for me, I will watch for the Lord. I will wait for the God Who saves me. My God will hear me.
MICAH 7:7

YOUR SHEPHERD

Brave Boy,

I am your Savior who lives forever. Because of My sacrifice on the cross, you also can have a joyful life that lasts forever. I am your Shepherd who leads you the right way. You don't need material things to make you happy and content—even though that's what the world would like you to believe. Rely on Me for everything, and you will find true and lasting joy.

I gave everything for you, brave one. Think about My love all day long. Trust Me, because I alone am worthy. I am not here to judge you. . .I came only to love. Know that whatever you do, even when you make mistakes, I love you and call you Mine. When you mess up, just ask for My forgiveness and you'll have it!

Just as I saved your life, I also give you

freedom from heavy burdens. I am pulling you closer to Me every hour of every day. Your sin can't build a wall between us because when you make a mistake and ask forgiveness, My love and mercy flow like a river from My heart to yours. Follow Me, your Shepherd. I will forgive you and take away your shame. Let Me show you how I take your regrets and shape them into a beautiful, hopeful future.

Our promise to You will be kept.
O You Who hears prayer,
to You all men come.
Psalm 65:1-2

EVERY PART OF YOU

Brave Boy,

From the very first rays of morning sun to the last hints of light in the evening sky, My love shines over you. My perfect beauty is reflected in all of creation. My zeal for you and your well-being is like a fire that can never be put out. I am your ultimate Protector. I have amazing plans for your life. You are so very important to Me, and I hold you close to My side. Let these truths fill your heart with gladness.

I want you to know that I will never leave you all alone. Don't let anyone or anything make you feel like I don't care. I love every part of you, and I care about everything you care about. I will always fight for you, child. Be still. Listen to My instructions. Read My words and feel My love surround you.

With each new day, I give you a fresh

start. Be willing to give up your own plans and dreams so that you are free to receive all the amazing blessings and plans I have for you. I always want what's best for you. Hear My gentle voice call you closer to Me. I have paid the highest price for your heart. Nothing more needs to be done for you to have your sins forgiven. You have been washed clean. You have been made brand-new!

I do not want to be proud of anything except in the cross of our Lord Jesus Christ. Because of the cross, the ways of this world are dead to me, and I am dead to them.

GALATIANS 6:14

MERCY AND GRACE

Brave Boy,

Do you ever feel like I'm not big enough to handle all your problems? Don't believe the lie that tells you I'm not strong enough to carry you through hard times. Child, let Me complete the good work I've started in you. You are so brave and strong because My power is in you! It's okay if you sometimes feel like you can't do great things. Just remember that I am leading you by the hand, and I'm never letting you go.

Our relationship is a promise based on love and forgiveness. Come close to Me. Don't stay away because you feel bad about making a mistake. That's why I'm here. That's why I went to the cross for you. I am your Savior and Friend. Call out to Me. I promise that I will always save you. In return, use your life to honor Me.

Let others know that My grace is waiting to forgive them too.

Love My instructions more than anything. Keep listening to My voice and let My words guide you. Stay in community with other believers. Use your words to give Me praise. Let the world hear your songs of thanks. Help your brothers and sisters in need. Let them see My love when they see you. Let your life be a beautiful reflection of My mercy and grace. That's what being brave is all about!

See what great love the Father has for us that He would call us His children. And that is what we are.
1 JOHN 3:1

MY FORGIVENESS

Brave Boy,

My love for you never fails. It overflows into your heart day after day after day. Even when you feel far from Me, I am here loving you. I am always with you. My love and care for you are unending, and I will never love you less because you make mistakes. Ask for My forgiveness. Know that I am working to help you become bold and courageous.

Each new day is an opportunity to walk closer with Me. Let Me show you brand-new, better ways of looking at the world. Let Me guide you. Feel Me wash away all your sins. My heart beats for you, brave boy. Use your freedom to bring Me glory by serving others. I will give you everything you need to do My good work.

From the time I created you, I have desired your whole heart. I have wanted to teach you wisdom. I have wanted you to talk to Me and share everything that's on your heart. I have wanted to carry all your burdens for you. Child, I don't hold grudges. That's not who I am. When you invited Me into your heart, you were made new. Even though you'll still make mistakes sometimes, I will forgive you when you ask. Trust that I will forgive you. My forgiveness cleans your heart and makes you whiter than the winter snow.

If we tell Him our sins, He is faithful and we can depend on Him to forgive us of our sins. He will make our lives clean from all sin.

I JOHN 1:9

MY UNFAILING LOVE

Brave Boy,

I am with you today. I will be with you forever. I will never turn away from you or forget about you. My Holy Spirit is within you, and that will never change. I love you and want to show you just how much you mean to Me. Today, I want you to experience more of Me. I have proved Myself faithful, so no matter what you're feeling, know that I am here to give you more of My unfailing love.

In this new day I have given you, find more hope. Know that I am here to bring you joy—the same joy you experienced on the day of your salvation. Today I will give you a willing spirit so you can be brave and strong. I am giving you grace to be My voice in this dark and broken world. Lead those who need Me back to the cross. Help them turn to Me.

Be courageous and tell the world that I am their Savior. Be in the habit of speaking My powerful name and telling those who will listen that I am here to break their chains of guilt. Let your words tell the story of My love for them. Let your tongue sing songs of My unfailing love for the brokenhearted. In the middle of trials, praise My name so the world will know I am King. Little one, what I want from you is a humble spirit and a heart that seeks Me forever.

The secret is this: Christ in you brings hope of all the great things to come.
COLOSSIANS 1:27

YOUR STRONGHOLD

Brave Boy,

Continue to live humbly and bravely. Serve your friends, family, and others. Tell them of My mighty name and all I have done for you. Tell others of My great love all day long so that they will come to see My love and mercy and so that their hearts may open to the gift of eternal life I offer them.

Bring hope to those who are sad, lonely, and weak. Don't let anything get in the way of sharing your story. You can bring light to the darkness—yes, you! I call you worthy because I saved your soul and made you a brand-new creation. You are special because you are Mine!

I am your strength. Keep believing in My promises and know I am here to protect you from the enemy's lies. Take the gift of today and build others up.

Help them find their worth in Me. Be bold. Tell them about My grace. Be brave and lead them to Me. Show them how I can rescue them. Use your words to bring hope to the hopeless. Use your life to bring grace to the lives of others. Let My Word be your guide. I am so proud of you!

**"God is my strong place.
He has made my way safe."**
2 SAMUEL 22:33

191

SHOW THEM

Brave Boy,

You are so important to Me. Your heart beats for Me, and that brings Me glory and delight. The world you live in is filled with people who don't believe I exist. Their hearts are being pulled farther and farther away from Me, because the enemy doesn't want anyone to know about My unending love.

If you know people who don't believe in Me, show them differently. Show them who I really am. Be truthful and real. Tell them how My grace saved you. Teach them how My sacrifice made a way for you to have a forever life in heaven someday. If you're feeling unsure of what to say, I will give you the right words. Keep being brave!

Never hesitate to show others the hope you have in Me. Let your words and actions be a picture of My love. Let others see how you treat all people with respect. Let them see how you show compassion for those in need. Let them feel My presence every time they are near you. Then they will know that I am inviting them into a relationship with Me too. Keep following Me. Brave one, you are wonderful to Me.

So the Lord wants to show you kindness. He waits on high to have loving-pity on you. For the Lord is a God of what is right and fair. And good will come to all those who hope in Him.
ISAIAH 30:18

Brave Boy,

Remember that I reached out to you first. I alone made a way for your salvation. Because of My mercy and grace, your sins have been washed away forever. So worship Me every day with a grateful heart. Don't just save your worship for church on Sundays. When you praise Me, I fill your soul with hope and joy. Daily worship brings you even closer to Me, brave one. Talk to Me. I hear your every word, and I love you so much!

What I did on the cross for you is truth! I loved you so much that I chose a criminal's death, even though I didn't deserve it. I shed My blood on the cross so you could be set free from the chains of sin. It's because of Me that you are truly alive. Because I love you, I hear every one of your prayers and forgive every one of your sins. Because I have chosen you, you stand before Me today unashamed and brand new! I am your Savior. I am your help, your hope. I am in control. You are safe with Me!

The mountains melt like a candle before the Lord, before the Lord of the whole earth.
PSALM 97:5

Brave Boy,

I hear your prayers. I listen to every single word. I care about what you have to say. Don't stop talking to Me. Tell Me everything and trust that I am here for you. The enemy wants you to think I ignore your prayers. But the truth is that you're My special creation and your heart is very precious to Me. I offer you love in your sadness. I offer you hope in your pain. And I offer you grace in your failing. I am listening, child, and I will answer you. Have faith in Me and don't forget that My mercy carries you between prayers as you wait on My answers.

I know you sometimes have doubts. But trust that I am here for you every minute of the day. Trust that you are loved and cared for, no matter what. You know that I call you My child. Don't let any doubts that creep into your thoughts erase your confidence in My love. Know that your heart is safe in My hands. Don't be downcast, brave one, because I have set you free!

The Lord is not slow about keeping His promise as some people think. He is waiting for you. The Lord does not want any person to be punished forever. He wants all people to be sorry for their sins and turn from them.

2 PETER 3:9

Brave Boy,

I know you go through times when you feel confused. I know you have moments when you feel like My forgiveness isn't strong enough to reach your heart. When you make mistakes, don't try to hide from Me. I didn't make you to run away, and I certainly didn't create you to hide your feelings from Me. I love you and want you to come near to Me. I want you to talk to Me. Don't forget how special you are, child.

When hard times come, don't focus on the storm. Instead, hold on to Me. I am here for you. And I am strong enough to handle all your troubles. In Me you will find rest and forgiveness. In Me alone you will find mercy and grace. Know that I am protecting your heart from the troubles the enemy puts in your way.

Don't be confused when people try to twist My words. Spend time in the Bible so you can understand Me and know the truth. Cling to your faith and hope in Me. This is how you will find true freedom for your life. In the middle of hard times, hold tight to Me and My words. I will never let go of you or let you down!

[Jesus] said to them, "Come away from the people. Be by yourselves and rest."
MARK 6:31

CLOSER TOGETHER

Brave Boy,

I know there are times when your heart feels overwhelmed from all the burdens you bear. Remember, child, I am here for you. I hear your cries for help. I am your King, and you are My treasure. I will carry you through every struggle. In tough times I will help you be strong and brave!

Keep your heart open to My promises. Don't try to handle your problems on your own. My love for you brings us closer together, and nothing can keep us apart. You are never a burden to Me. You are not a mistake. You are My beloved child, and you are forgiven. I know how hard life can be sometimes, but don't forget that I am here and will give you peace.

Your feelings change, but I am always the same. Whether you're feeling happy, sad, angry, silly, or stressed out, I never change. I am here today, and I love you just the same as I did yesterday. Rest in this truth, brave one. Find peace in My words. You are Mine forever. I am your Savior and your Lord. I made you for My glory, and I never make mistakes!

"I am the Bread of Life. He who comes to Me will never be hungry. He who puts his trust in Me will never be thirsty."
JOHN 6:35

NEVER ALONE

Brave Boy,

You matter to Me. I am your King, and you are My wonderful creation. I know you have struggles and worries throughout the day. But think of My love as a big iron shield all around your heart. It will protect you from harm. It will keep you free from worry. Nothing can get through the shield of My love, brave one.

No matter what someone might say about you, no matter what someone might do to try to hurt your heart, I am here to comfort you. You are not alone to face this day. You are not alone to solve all your problems. Trust Me. I am with you and we will face this new day together. Through My wisdom and strength, you will find answers and you will be blessed.

Spend time today reading My Word. Make choices that will make Me proud. Don't be afraid of anything, because nothing anyone can say or do matters more than My love for you. Quiet your heart, tune out the noise of the world, and just listen for My voice. Brave one, I love you from the moment you open your eyes in the morning until the time you go to sleep at night. . .and I love you every minute in between. Nothing can keep Me away from you.

"But who do you say that I am?"
MARK 8:29

COVERED IN MY LOVE

Brave Boy,

I am *for* you! I want only the best for you. And I will always have your back. I experience everything you experience. I feel everything you feel. I care about the things you care about. Oh, how I am for you, brave one! Every moment and every emotion you experience, I am with you through it all.

Each joy that rises in your heart and each tear that drips down your cheek is known by Me, your loving Creator. Reread My promises in the Bible and you'll understand that I am here for you. I will give ou rest when you need it. I will help you find the truth when you have questions. Have faith in Me and know that I am strong enough and I love you enough to see you through this day. Nothing will harm you because you are safe in My arms.

When you feel unloved, find comfort

in My Word. Know that I love you immeasurably. When you feel sad, know that I am here to lift your head and protect your heart from the enemy's attacks. Keep trusting in Me and My words. Believe Me when I say I'm holding you close to My heart. On days when you're waiting for Me to answer, I will help you turn your fears into praise. Your belief in Me destroys worry. You can't possibly feel sad when you're covered in My love. And nothing can diminish My love for you. Not one thing.

We had broken the Law many ways. Those sins were held against us by the Law. That Law had writings which said we were sinners. But now He has destroyed that writing by nailing it to the cross.
COLOSSIANS 2:14

JUST SAY MY NAME

Brave Boy,

Don't hold anything back from Me. Don't hold anything in. Know that you are safe when you share your thoughts and feelings with Me. I am here for you, day or night. I will always care for you because you are My child. Live your life like I want you to live it. Obey My Word. Live in My love.

When the troubles of this world are overwhelming, remember that I am all you'll ever need. I died for you so you can live free and forgiven. When your heart feels empty, remember that it's My love for you that will fill up every little space to make it overflow with joy again.

When you need Me, just say My name. I am the One who defends you, the One who guards your life and walks through every disaster with you. I give you safety and protection. Stay with Me. I am covering you in My love. And whenever you need it, I offer you My forgiveness. When you feel tired or weak or burdened by much sadness, My love will save you every time. I will show you endless mercy, nonstop faithfulness. You are wonderful to Me!

The Law says that almost everything is made clean by blood. Sins are not forgiven unless blood is given.

HEBREWS 9:22

THE ULTIMATE PRICE

Brave Boy,

Let every step you take bring you closer to telling those around you that I am their Savior. Tell others they can't save themselves. Remind them that no one but Me can give them life that goes on forever. No price can buy My salvation. I alone paid the ultimate price for every person in the world. Share that I am the only Answer. My love is the greatest treasure in the world. I'm proud of your faith in Me, brave one. I'm thankful you have My heart for people!

Read your Bible every day to gain more understanding. Let My words soak into your soul. Let My promises be your source of strength. They will remain your shelter in a world of uncertainty. When you face difficult times, I will lift you out of despair and carry you to beautiful, safe pastures of peace. Follow Me and you will find the rest and renewal you need.

I am your King. I call you out of your comfortable routine and send you out to tell the world about Me. Remember that I don't need anything you have to offer—I only want you and your wonderful heart. No matter how you feel today, trust that I am your loving heavenly Father and you are My beloved child. My feelings for you will never change.

We are sure that if we ask anything that He wants us to have, He will hear us.
I John 5:14

NO PRIDE

Brave Boy,

Remember Me when you have trouble. Read My Word and you'll understand more about Me. You'll know more about My love and care for you. You'll learn you can trust Me in every area of your life! Believe Me when I say you are forgiven and that I forget your sins. Call out to Me anytime, day or night. Know that when I look at you, I see Myself reflected in your beautiful smile.

I have given you a brand-new life. So rejoice and be glad, brave one! Come close to Me. Remember all the promises I have made to you. I wash away your sins so your heart is pure and clean. I renew your spirit so it is strong again. I promise to forgive you each time you confess your sins, and I always keep My word. You are a treasure to Me, and I love you.

Stay with Me and grow into the amazing young man I created you to be. Keep trusting in Me and My never-ending love. Think about My faithfulness and all I've done for you. I will keep you strong for My glory. Through every minute of this day, hope in Me alone. I am calling you to do work for My kingdom, and I will give you everything you need to succeed. Don't ever doubt that I am in control. I will never leave you!

"Because of this, I say to you, whatever you ask for when you pray, have faith that you will receive it. Then you will get it."
MARK 11:24

SATISFIED WITH ME

Brave Boy,

People who don't know Me are afraid of so many things. But you can help by sharing Me and My love with them—and showing them that they don't need to be afraid of anything if they invite Me into their lives. Show them how much you care about them. And tell them that I am standing at the door of their hearts, waiting to rescue their souls. When they give their lives to Me, rejoice and be glad! You are My wonderful child, and I am so proud of you!

I know you are surrounded by people who don't believe in Me. Don't let their behavior discourage you from chasing after Me. Stay focused on My truth. Don't spend your time worrying. Instead, praise Me because I am good. Praise Me because I have delivered you from all your troubles. Don't spend your freedom chaining yourself back to sin. Grace is who you are now. Remember that I love you and that you are Mine, forever!

I know that today may seem overwhelming, but stay near Me, child. I love you and have planned only the very best for your life. Take comfort in the blessings I give you. Be satisfied with Me and the plans I have for you. You have been set free to follow Me. Be brave always.

"But be glad and have joy forever in what I make."
ISAIAH 65:18

PEACE IN THE PLAN

Brave Boy,

Let Me continue molding you into the person I made you to be. Living in a broken world means you will sometimes have hard days. Keep your eyes open for My blessings. Be joyful. Go about your day with an open heart. Be brave because I am always here to help you. I am here to show you the right way, and I will give you the strength you need to succeed. I have good plans for you, wonderful plans to use your life to bring glory to My name.

I am continually filling you with My goodness. Even on your very bad days I am filling you with grace. I am with you today, and I will be with you tomorrow and every day after that. Don't listen when the enemy tries to tell you that you are not worthy of My awesome plans. Remember, I made you—and I don't make mistakes!

So, brave one, find peace in My perfect plans for your life. I have appointed you to accomplish specific tasks, because I have gifted you to do them like no one else can. You are so special to Me! I am your King forever, and I will never stop guiding you. Keep your eyes and your heart fixed on Me.

"Yes, if you ask anything in My name, I will do it."
JOHN 14:14

OVERFLOWING WITH HOPE

Brave Boy,

When you feel lost and confused, chase after Me. When you feel unloved, call My name. I didn't create you for sadness. No. I created you for hope! I created you for confidence and expectation! Open your Bible and read My promises. Let Me give you strength and fill your heart to overflowing with hope. You are loved. You are special. And you are Mine. Just ask Me to rescue you. . .and then watch Me save you from the doubts and unhappy feelings. In Me, you are forgiven!

I sit on My throne and listen to everything you have to say. Don't let anything in the world make you doubt My love. Instead, spend your days praising Me. Hand every bit of stress and worry over to Me. I am here to carry you through hard times. I will not let you be shaken.

You can trust Me!

Trust in My promises. Every one of them is for your good. I love you, and I don't want to see you sad and burdened. When your prayers seem to go unanswered, remember all I have already done for you. Remember that I gave you My life, and when you accepted Me, you became a new creation. I am strong enough to carry you and all your burdens. Remember how much I love you, and rest in My faithfulness.

We will receive from Him whatever we ask if we obey Him and do what He wants.
I JOHN 3:22

Brave Boy,

Keep your thoughts on Me and My perfect plans for you. Simply think of Me and let your heart be filled with thanks that I went to the cross for you. When the enemy tries to confuse your thoughts, remember that I rescued you. In Me, you will never stumble. In Me, you will have lasting light in the darkness. You are a brand-new creation, and you are Mine. I am by your side every single day. You are not alone, and best of all, I will never stop loving you!

Instead of thinking about your mistakes today, keep your thoughts on My love and grace. Stay close to Me. Let your heart beat in praise, not fear. I am your Savior who never walks away. I am not like man, whose heart is full of selfishness and pride. I am not like man, who will break promises.

Rest assured that I will never bring you harm. I have saved you from sin and restored you to a right relationship with Me. You have no need to seek fulfillment anywhere but in Me. Only I can satisfy your deepest longings. Only I can bring you lasting joy. No one loves you like I do—I gave everything for you! When you trust Me, you can know how much you are loved and needed.

I can do all things because Christ gives me the strength.
PHILIPPIANS 4:13

Brave Boy,

Today, tomorrow, and all your days, I will help you. I will keep you from falling. I will remind you that even though the world's kingdoms fall, I am always lifting you up. Concentrate on My goodness. Remember that I am faithful. I am just. I am trustworthy. Listen to My voice and hear the new song of mercy I have for you. My words will melt away your stress and fear.

Don't be nervous. Don't fear the future. Remain brave and focus on the fact that with Me, you are courageous. I will always be with you. Even when you make mistakes, I won't walk away. I will *never* leave you. When you sin and the devil is there to declare you a failure, I am there to shout that you've been forgiven. When you make a choice that you know is wrong, I don't love you any less. I will remove your shame. I am here to forgive.

I am going ahead of you to lead the way, so have no fear. I will protect you from the enemy's traps. He can't reach you here in the shadow of My wings. I delight in you! Be confident that you are My wonderful creation and that I have great things in store for you. Stay close to Me and shine bright. You are brave and amazing to Me!

For the Lord loves what is fair and right. He does not leave the people alone who belong to Him. They are kept forever. But the children of the sinful will be cut off.
PSALM 37:28

MORE GREAT BOOKS
for Brave Boys!

100 Adventurous Stories for Brave Boys

Boys are history-makers! And this deeply compelling storybook proves it! This collection of 100 adventurous stories of Christian men—from the Bible, history, and today—will empower you to know and understand how men of great character have made an impact in the world and how much smaller our faith (and the biblical record) would be without them.

Hardback / 978-1-64352-356-9 / $16.99

Cards of Character for Brave Boys: Shareable Devotions and Encouragement

You'll discover just who God made you to be with these tear-out, shareable Cards of Character, featuring important messages that boys like you need to hear!

Paperback / 978-1-64352-736-9 / $7.99

The Bible for Brave Boys

Part of the exciting Brave Boys series, this Bible provides complete Old and New Testament text in the easy-reading New Life™ Version, plus insert pages featuring full-color illustrations of bold, adventurous men such as Abraham, Moses, Joshua, David, Daniel, Peter, and, of course, Jesus!

DiCarta / 978-1-64352-528-0 / $24.99

With your parent's permission, check out www.forbraveboys.com where you'll discover additional positive, faith-building activities and resources!

BARBOUR
kidz
A Division of Barbour Pub